KON

Editorials

Articles

Cover art: Sherlock and Professor Challenger face the Martian Menace; art by Jolyon Yates
Page 4 & 59: art by Andy Ross

Brian Harris, Editor & Publisher • **Tony Strauss**, Editor & Proofing
Timothy Paxton, Editor, Publisher & Lay Out/Design

LET IT SNOW, LET IT SNOW, LET IT--
CAN YOU DO BETTER THAN THIS, MAN?

The holidays are upon us, once again, and Weng's Chop has released another holiday spooktacular! The month of October, November and December are the busiest times of the year, so what better way to kick back and take some time out for yourself then to crack open WC magazine? You're guaranteed to get tricks, treats, turkeys getting stuffed, and a fat guy emptying his sack (of glad tidings)! Oh and there's also a few movie reviews and articles!

Seeing as how this will be our last WC for the year 2015, I only feel it's fair to ask the question, what in the hell did you enjoy watching this season year? What were some of your favorite films, be they horror, exploitation, science fiction, fantasy, or even porn? Whether it was made and released in 2015 on screens or VOD or made 30 years ago and just now hitting disc in 2015, what did you find to be the greatest viewing experience of this year? Our upcoming issue 9 of WC will be presenting lists for writers and filmmakers answering this very question. Hopefully you return for WC 9 and check those lists out.

On the news front, the cat is officially out of the bag and Troy Howarth has been signed to Wildside-Kronos Publications for a single book deal! Soon we will have a super cool filmography featuring the films of the incomparable actor/monster/hedonist extraordinaire, Klaus Kinski (*Real Depravities: The Films of Klaus Kinski*). We here at Wildside-Kronos are very excited and we are positive you are going to love this book. We'll be sure to keep you updated.

With so much drama going in the online realm and terror in the world around us, I truly hope all of you stay safe and enjoy your holidays with family and friends. Give gifts, be merry and always remember to read WC and Monster. Oh, and yes, I am still accepting drugs as payment for this magazine, so don't be stingy on the "snow," Father Winter, and I'll have a few copies out to you as soon as possible. (*Dude...I'm good for it, you know I'm good for it dammit, don't act like I'm not good for it. Whenever I say spot me, I always get you back and you know this...why are you acting like I'm going to stiff you? Shit man I thought we were boys. Alright I see how it is, I see. Yeah, Merry F'in' Christmas to you too, Grinch!*)
~*Brian Harris*

CANDY'S BEEN EATEN AND TURKEY NAP'S OVER—
WHERE'S MY PRESENTS?!

Season's Greetings to all you festive freaks and furry fornicators out there in Cinemaland! Another year is coming to a close, and we at *Weng's Chop* want nothing more than to spend the remainder of it with you, cuddled up by the fire, roasting chestnuts and sipping hot cocoa, watching some seriously strange movies together. So that's what we're gonna goddamn do. Sorry, but you have no choice in the matter, so just come to terms with it and let it happen.

So here we are with our third holiday Spooktacular Special: the annual digest-sized edition that proudly fucks up your bookshelf's uniformity (and your OCD) when stacked up chronologically with our other issues (and just to keep things extra annoying, we make sure it's not even the same size as *Monster!* digest. Take that, society!) and continues to throw off our issue numbering ever more each year (this is number 8.5, which naturally means it is the twelfth issue of *Weng's Chop*). As always, and as befits the title, we're loaded to the gills with (mostly) spooky-themed stuff to keep your winter nights restless and your heebie-jeebies at their absolute heebiest. But if you're easily frightened, fear not...there's some other non-horror stuff mixed in, too, so there's fun for pathetic little wussies, as well. Hell, even if you're all stuck up and don't wanna cuddle with us by the fire with chestnuts and cocoa (as if you could resist us), this issue is a perfect year-end companion to keep next to the toilet to read while you do your most important work.

As we roll into the New Year, we're going to be comin' at you strong (*ew!*) with all kinds of Wildside-Kronos Wonderments™, so you'd best be ready! Aside from the regular monthly onslaught of *Monster!* digest, we'll very shortly be releasing the long-awaited return of *Monster! International*...nearly two years in the making, this mammoth-sized volume of long-form reviews and articles of a monstrous nature is nearly finished, and will be headed your way just after the New Year's bell tolls. Thick enough to boost a baby on a barstool, this sucker is gonna knock your ever-lovin' socks off, and will prove itself to be well worth the wait.

Then, in late February/early March, we'll be throwing *Weng's Chop* #9 at'cha, another book-thick issue which is already a-bubblin' and a-boilin' with some high-proof interviews and articles that we can't wait to announce. We're also excited to say that once again, this and all foreseeable editions of *Weng's Chop* will offer both the regularly priced **Standard Edition** and the aptly named **More Expensive Color Edition** options, which we shall continue to offer as long as you continue to respond so positively to it. Seriously, we're so damned happy that y'all like it, because we're in love with the way the More Expensive Color Edition Experiment of 2015™ came out, and genuinely feel it's worth the exorbitant cost of the color printing process. But again, we stress that we have absolutely *no* plans of *EVER* stopping our beloved black-and-white **Standard Edition**.

As my handsome and learned colleague Brian Harris already mentioned, we are also thrilled to be releasing our first actual *book* book, *Real Depravities: The Films of Klaus Kinski*, by Troy Howarth, esteemed author of *Splintered Visions: Lucio Fulci and His Films*, *So Deadly, So Perverse: 50 Years of Italian Giallo Films* and *The Haunted World of Mario Bava*, as well as a cherished member of our *Weng's Chop/Monster!* family. Troy's working like a madman on meth at this project, and we can already tell it's going to be something special. More on this as it develops.

What Mr. Harris did *not* mention—perhaps due to modesty, perhaps due to PCP ingestion—is that work has begun on a floor-to-ceiling overhauled, revised 2nd edition of his acclaimed book *filmBRAWL*, which is going to be so amazing that you're likely to immediately set fire to your beloved first edition and hurl it into the fiery pits of Tallahassee. (Or, perhaps more wisely, sell that old edition on eBay, 'cause that shit's outta print, yo!) At any rate, we hope to have that pugilistic beast set loose on you sometime in 2016, as well, but to whet your appetite, we've included a special sneak preview of it in this very issue!

We've got some other pretty awesome projects on the workbench also, though nothing set firm enough in stone to drop any promises yet (but stay tuned, because *damn!*)...but all in all, 2016 is looking to be fulla Wildside-Kronos Goodness™. With a year of monthly *Monster!*s, a quartet (gods willing) of *Weng's Chop*s, and a pair o' books on the way, we'd like to humbly request at least 18 spaces on your cinema book shelf next year, please!

In the meantime, we'd like to thank you wonderful readers for spending 2015 with us, and hope that your holiday season is safe, warm and full of love. I'd also like to thank all of our outstanding contributors for another year of stellar work...you guys and gals are fucking awesome, and we love you all in ways that are highly inappropriate and probably unsanitary.

We'll see you all next year! *SMEWCH!* Mistletoe, bitches!
~*Tony Strauss*

THE HORROR OF THE HOLYDAZE
Gods bless ya - every last one of ye basterds ~ *Tim Paxton*

This page: The devil snacks on souls in Disney's *Hell's Bells*
Opposite page: A COMPANY OF WOLVES ... see page 78

ELEMENTARY, MY DEAR WHATSIT:
SHERLOCK HOLMES VS. THE RED PLANET MARS
Or: The Rats Are Coming!
The Bayou Babes Are Here! Part 2

by Stephen R. Bissette

In the last volume of Weng's Chop, *I wrote about Manly Wade Wellman, his son Wade Wellman, and* Sherlock Holmes's War of the Worlds *(Warner Books, 1975), their revisionist Sherlock Holmes adventure featuring Professor Challenger in a lively fusion of Sir Arthur Conan Doyle, Herbert George Wells, and the "martian" invasion of Earth at the end of the 19th and 20th centuries—all in the context of the current 21st century War of the Worlds revival we're in.*

This brings us to the second phase of this curious fusion of Doyle and Wells, Holmes and Mars, in a far less heady publishing ghetto of the 1960s and 1970s paperback science fiction marketplace than Manley Wade Wellman and Son worked within.

Ahem.

Have you ever heard of George H. Smith?

Because, you see, there was more than one George H. Smith, and we might need a Holmes before we're done to sort out which George Smith is which, and who it might have been who truly dragged Holmes into another confrontation with the martian invaders.

This is, in and of itself, a bit of a detective tale, as you will see. *The game's afoot!*

The George Smith, writer, I'm concerned with here is one George *Henry* Smith.

George *Henry* Smith is not to be confused with science fiction author George O. Smith, nor with the other, somewhat notorious and definitively naughty George H. Smith.

George Henry Smith was prolific, to say the least. He had lots of science fiction short stories published in the newsstand SF digests and pulps of the 1950s and '60s, including "The Ordeal of Colonel Johns" (*If Worlds of Science Fiction*, June 1954, Vol. 2, No. 4; cover art by Edward Valigursky), "Too Robot to Marry" (*Fantastic Universe*, October 1959, Vol. 11, No. 6) on through to work in *Famous Science Fiction Tales of Wonder* (first issue!, Winter 1966/67; cover art by Virgil Finley), "In the Land of Love" (*Worlds of Tomorrow* #24, 1970 Vol. 5, No. 1; cover by Jack Gaughan, who has a part to play in this conversation), and many more.[1]

The Holy Grail for George H. Smith fans: *Paperback Parade* #36, October 1993 (scan from the SpiderBaby Archives—i.e., the author's collection)

---

1   Since completion of this article and final proofing, I've discovered new material on the George H. Smith mystery, including a 1993 published interview with George *Henry* Smith. I will use these footnotes to incorporate as much new information as I can without driving my *WC* editors insane. In that 1993 interview, Smith reveals that "the first story I sold was a science fiction short named 'The Last Spring' to *Startling Stories* in about 1952 or 1953. The second was to *Wonder Stories*. I got in at the end of the pulps and wrote stories of many different kinds. I did SF, Detective, Love, Western, Western Romances and War fiction published. I sold hundreds of short shorts, short stories and articles to science fiction magazines, men's magazines, war magazines, detective magazines and what have you before I ever did a book. I used to write all or almost all of one so-called 'true war stories' for a couple of the true war magazines..." ("An Interview with George H. Smith" by Gary Lovisi, *Paperback Parade* #36, October 1993, pp. 39-40).

IT CAN HAPPEN HERE!

50c
EPIC ✱ BOOK
NO. 103

1976

A Sensational Story Of Terror and Sadism As Ruthless Mobs Battle The Secret Police In The United States Of Tomorrow!

OF

BY GEORGE SMITH

"Mob hell! The Libertarians have been preaching for twenty years and we've had three of them in power. So now they're finally going to get anarchy. But it won't be the kind they're looking for. They've created an anarchy for the powerful and rich only..." George H. Smith, *1976: Year of Terror* (Epic Books, 1961)

Bear with me, now. This will be fun, and it will provide a snapshot (for the uninitiated) of just how crazy the paperback publishing world used to be—and how abundant paperback originals were for about three to four decades. George Henry Smith and George H. Smith (and, for that matter, George O. Smith) were right in the thick of it, and it's now up to anyone who cares to try and sort it all out.

Lucky you—*I care.*

The earliest George *Henry* Smith SF paperback novel I've stumbled upon is the curious *1976: Year of Terror* (Epic Books, 1961), which I'll talk about in some detail later.

Suffice to say for now that it was a rough item in its day, a vision of North America *"under a reign of terror by the Libertarian Party and the Secret Police...Mobs of hot rodders and winos roam the streets, looting, killing, raping!"*

Yes, you read that right.

Them goddamned Libertarians!

Who knew they'd play such a central role in the utter collapse of the American way of life?

George Henry Smith knew, that's who!

Believe it or not (believe it), Smith was simply tossing his hat into an already popular paperback original genre, and one Tea Party members of today might find rewarding to revisit. Hell, it might provide a proper platform for 'em. And *1976: The Year of Terror* still reads like a Fox News wet dream, and has about the same tenuous grasp on politics, science, fiction, and the difference between them.[2]

This was a contemporary of the Ray Milland-helmed and -starring vehicle **PANIC IN YEAR ZERO!** (1962), which was novelized by none other than Dean Owen—author of the racy Monarch Books novelizations of **THE BRIDES OF DRACULA** (1960), **KONGA** and **REPTILICUS** (both 1961). **PANIC IN YEAR ZERO!** was novelized as *End of the World* (1962, Ace Books). *End of the World*'s cover copy summed it up:

> *"When the H-bombs struck America, they wiped out not only the cities but law and order and inhibitions. The few who remained alive were faced with the fierce fight for survival."*

Given firearm sales since the 2008 election, I reckon *End of the World* is making the rounds again (pun intended). Both novels were—well, they still *are*, to be concise (in 21st Century terms)—Tea Party survivalist wish-ful-

George made the cut in anthologies like *The First World of IF: 20 Outstanding Short Stories from the First Five Years of IF Science Fiction Magazine* (1957, Quinn Publishing, cover by Mel Hunter), *Now and Beyond* (1965, Belmont Books, featuring Smith's story "The Outcasts"), and *Body Armor 2000* (1986, Ace Books, with Smith's "The Last Crusade"), among others.

George Henry Smith was also a fairly prolific paperback original SF author, too, and this is where the confusion sets in.

Because, you see, there was *another* super-prolific George H. Smith grinding out adult paperbacks even as George Henry Smith was writing his often adult SF paperback originals. But the *other* George H. Smith's adult paperback novels were far, far racier and raunchier than anything I've read by George *Henry* Smith.

Jeez, and I thought my late amigo Steve Perry had problems with this kind of mixup (his work was always being confused with one of the other Steve Perrys of the world, including prolific and still-writing SF author Steve Perry).

2   George Henry Smith on this novel: "*1976 The Year of Terror* was a kind of hobby horse of mine that I could never sell to a straight publisher. I added a little sex when [editor/publisher] David Zentner of Epic needed a book. It was published although I don't imagine it sold very well..." ("An Interview with George H. Smith" by Gary Lovisi, *Paperback Parade* #36, October 1993, p9. 38-39).

fillment fantasy in its purest form. As I just mentioned, these novels display the contemporary GOP/GOTea grasp of science at work: radiation is, uh, somewhere *"over there"—you* know, where the bombs went off, and manageably avoided even after nuclear Armageddon.

Patriarchs are unquestionably in charge, the more cold-blooded and ruthless the better, as long as they keep their own family's needs first; women are frails—to be protected at all costs from their own socialist instincts and from roving rapist renegades— quivering in the wake of civilization's collapse, but essential for mating and mothering surviving children and teens. It's a tough world, post-apocalypse, but armed with stern patriotic machismo, unflagging ire, and sufficient firepower (guns, rifles, and dry ammo are *all-important*), the American patriarch may yet survive to rebuild.

This places George Henry Smith on the cutting edge of early 1960s survivalist post-apocalyptic sleaze science-fiction, which provided a neat context for his revisionist *War of the Worlds* novel—which, yes, I am going to get to.

Smith's *The Four Day Weekend* (1966) warned, *"Cars are Taking Over Our Cities. Tomorrow – Our Lives!"* The novel was a fairly entertaining and engaging expansion of celebrated SF/ horror writer (who was also a professional doctor specializing in psychology) David H. Keller's first-ever published story, "The Revolt of the Pedestrians" (*Amazing Stories*, February 1928).[3] Keller posited a future in which pedestrians were essentially animals in a world dominated by automobiles; Smith's *The Four Day Weekend* depicted that takeover in broad, pulpish strokes in a slightly futuristic downtown Los Angeles, concluding with his protagonist and a ragtag team of beat poet/artists defeating the alien-controlled overmind orchestrating the auto rebellion. *The Four-Day Weekend* also reads as a lively precursor to Stephen King's short story "Trucks" (*Cavalier*, June 1973, reprinted in King's *Night Shift*, 1978), the TV movie adaptation **TRUCKS** (1997), and King's sole feature film directorial outing from his own script, **MAXIMUM OVERDRIVE** (1986).

But it's Smith's Mars novels I want to bring to your attention, given their connection with H.G. Wells' classic *War of the Worlds.*

Mars attacked Earth—in a way—in an earlier Smith novel, *The Unending Night* (1964), published in the US by Derby, CT-based Charlton Comics-related paperback publisher Monarch Books. Monarch was the publisher of the racy paperback novelizations of **KONGA, GORGO** (1961), **REPTILICUS**, etc. Yep, they cranked out original SF paperbacks, too, and George Henry Smith was in their price range.

"Mad with power, the scientist launched Mars on a collision course with earth!"

The cover was by Ralph Brillhart, which was a beaut, and as the back cover ballyhooed, *"It started with a runaway chain reaction in a gigantic thermonuclear power plant on Mars."* In the George Henry Smith universe, if it wasn't the fucking Libertarians, it was the whole of Red Planet Mars trying to crush the American way of life!

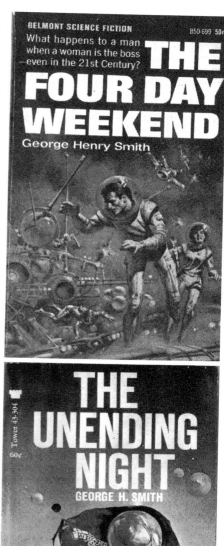

Mad with power, the scientist launched Mars on a collision course with earth.

A Big T Science Fiction

Top: George Henry Smith's *The Four Day Weekend* (Belmont, 1966) was a cautionary tale: "Cars are Taking Over Our Cities. Tomorrow – Our Lives!" **Above:** Jeff (Catherine) Jones cover art, *The Unending Night* (1964, Tower Books edition)

---

3   *The Four Day Weekend* also recalls aspects of Theodore Sturgeon's 1944 novella *Killdozer* (*Astounding*, November 1944; revised by Sturgeon for collection in the anthology *Aliens 4*, 1959) which was also adapted into a TV movie and to comics (*Worlds Unknown #6*, Marvel Comics) in 1974.

The same year's Tower Books edition (?) featured a cover by Jeff Jones, which was pretty sweet, too—though how there were *two* editions the same year from publishers only a few miles apart is in and of itself pretty curious (there was *also* a Priory Books edition, too).

Rest assured there were more than just two or three apocalyptic scenarios streaming through George Henry Smith's brain cells, though. This is just the tip of the iceberg (and I'll be saving the "best", and most influential, for last—so hold on to your firepower, folks). George Henry Smith was on *fire*, ladies and gentlemen, and the world had to know what we were in for!

I wouldn't be surprised to learn one of the potential cataclysms we were due to weather was sparked by how fast Smith's fingers blazed over those Underwood typewriter keys.

A year earlier, Monarch had published Smith's *Doomsday Wing* (1963), *"A Harrowing Tale of a World Gone Mad and on the Brink of Total Destruction!"*, sporting cover art by Earl Mayan. I'm not sure what that particular apocalypse involved, as I've yet to see the book itself and there's precious little online about it.

So, yes—Mars. Back to Mars.

Holmes.

The point of all this.

Yep, George Henry Smith brought Red Planet hellfire *back* on our heads in the 1970s.

Alas, *The Second War of the Worlds* (1976) is guaranteed to disappoint most fans and devotees of the 1898 H.G. Wells novel; nor is Smith even remotely in the world-class realm of Manly Wade Wellman and Wade Wellman.

In fact, there's a dearth of H.G. Wells and Sir Arthur Conan Doyle at work in *The Second War of the Worlds*. Smith spends most of his page count spinning his *own* unique fantasy (and I do mean fantasy, as opposed to science-fiction) of a world parallel to Earth, Annwn. This is a case of a writer dedicated to one path of personal fantastic fiction—Smith's Annwn fantasy/SF series—shoehorning a personal work into a more commercial, marketable format, peddled as a nominal sequel to *The War of the Worlds*. Annwn, even when it's being invaded by Martians (and Smith's martians *are* Martians, unlike Wellman and Wellman's revisionist Wells spinoff), is spiced with far more magic, telepathy, telekinesis, and period high adventure tropes (including a skirmish with a savage tribe on Annwn's equivalent of the Amazon) than Martians.

Smith's hero and heroine—the psychically devoted but eternally bickering couple of Scotsman Dylan McBride and his witch fiancée Carlinda—were the anchors of

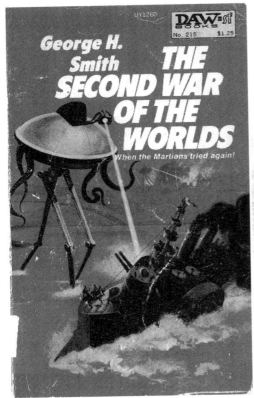

Cover and interior illustration art by Jack Gaughan for George Henry Smith's *The Second War of the Worlds* (Daw Books, 1976), delineating the novel's H.G. Wells Martian war machines and ignoring completely the meat of the book, Smith's invented Celtic proto-steampunk Annwn universe.

this quintet of revisionist Victorian fantasy/science-fiction novels, all of which spun abundant gears meshing a plethora of period genre concepts, characters, lifts and spinoffs. Their adventures remain a relatively unknown and unsung arc of alternative world fantasy/SF/adventure that some of you might find rewarding, apart from all the tomfoolery I'll be dancing around.

While I was never particularly enamored with the Annwn novels, I *did* read them all as they came out—but, my tastes being as utterly debased as they are, I only held on to the trashier SF Smith wrote in the early 1960s and *The Second War of the Worlds*, due to its Wells/Doyle curio factor.

So, let's sort all this out.

First of all, it must be noted that the Annwn novels are far superior to Smith's earlier original SF paperback works. His heart was clearly in the creation of the Annwn parallel-worlds universe and cast of characters, and his writing chops were sharper. There's a nice period flavor at work here, and by my reading, these were by far Smith's most inventive and most likely his most personal works. Had the term "steampunk" existed in 1976, Smith's Annwn novels might have proven even more marketable on their own terms.

Sans the steampunk label, Smith still didn't do too badly by Annwn, and vice-versa. The first book in the Annwn series was *Druids' World* (1967), followed by *Witch Queen of Lochlann* (Signet, 1969), *Kar Kaballa*—published in 1969 as an Ace Double-Back with Lin Carter's *Tower of the Medusa* with cover art John Schoenherr (Carter's novel is blessed by cover art credited by some to Jeff Jones, and others to Kelly Freas; it was most definitely the work of Jeff Jones).[4]

This trio was followed by *The Second War of the Worlds* (1976; cover art by Jack Gaughan), the book in which Smith dragged Sherlock Holmes, Dr. Watson and H.G. Wells' novel *War of the Worlds* into the Annwn parallel-worlds mix.

Gaughan also contributed one pen-and-ink interior illustration to the book, and it's a nifty if undistinguished piece. FYI, Jack Gaughan was a well-known SF illustrator of the period, having won a Hugo in 1967 for his work for the SF digests *Galaxy* and *If*; he was very active in SF circles for a couple of decades, and deserves some attention (far more than I can offer here). I recall his contribution to *Galaxy*'s initial publication of Cordwainer Smith's "The Last Castle" (*Galaxy*, April 1966), which helped my poor wee junior high school brain grasp the complex dynamic between characters (if memory serves, there was even a sort of "family tree" chart by Gaughan to help make sense of it all).

The Island Snatchers (DAW Books, 1978) by George Henry Smith, the fifth entry in the Annwn proto-steampunk novel series. Cover by Josh Kirby

So, is *The Second War of the Worlds* worth reading?

Well, yes. It's a lightweight entertainment, but there's some fun to be had here. It may even be that the entire Annwn series is richly deserving of rediscovery and reprinting now that steampunk is a vital, definable genre. Not being a steampunk devotee, per se, I found less meat to sink my teeth into than I discovered revisiting the Wellman & Son collaborative novel. As is obvious, I didn't find *The Second War of the Worlds* nearly as compelling, engaging and provocative as the Wellman/Wellman revisionist *Sherlock Holmes's War of the Worlds*, but let's face it: not many writers were in Wellman's ballpark, period. Nevertheless, I particularly recommend *The Second War of the Worlds* to Holmes completists, who by and large either remain ignorant of the book, or have willfully ignored it. Maybe they wish it never existed.

I'm frankly surprised so little is made of Sherlock Holmes and Watson's appearance and role here; they're *far* more involved in the novel than the Martians or any Wellsian characters, which rarely command center-stage. Smith is coy about their identities—"Dr. W" and "Mr. H" serve (along with the usual *"Elementary"* quips) to tag them as Conan Doyle's famous duo. It's more likely that the novel is just beneath the notice of Holmes devotees, given Smith's rep and confusion with the "other" paperback Smiths.

---

4 As of September 18th, 2010, Jeff/Catherine Jones personally confirmed absolutely that *The Unending Night* cover and the Lin Carter *Tower of the Medusa* were both CJ's handiwork; and, as an aside, that the publishers habitually gave artists no reference, description or details for the book the cover art was to accompany. My thanks to Catherine/Jeff—who, sadly, passed away soon after our FB message exchange.

That, at least, I can try to clear up here. But first…

There was a fifth George Henry Smith steampunk novel. Smith's sequel to *The Second War of the Worlds* was *The Island Snatchers* (DAW Books, 1978), "a new adventure set on Earth's twin, Annwn, which has only recently repulsed H.G. Wells's invaders from the red planet and is now forced to deal with the scoundrels that dared to snatch an entire island". I read it while I was at the Kubert School, but my copy is long lost and gone, and I'm sorry to say my memory isn't sharp enough to say much about it. The bookseller who used to have a copy available at *abebooks.com* going by the name MyBookieJoint liked it, writing *"The Island Snatchers* is a wonderful, whacky and adventurous tale, replete with Little People, lost races, and super-scientific perils."[5]

Now, there's a *lot* of confusion out there about George H. Smith. In fact, for most contemporary readers, it's damn near impossible to fathom how any one author could have written as many books as George H. Smith did— even knowing, as we think we do, there were *two* George H. Smiths, it's still almost impossible to grasp how much these two men wrote in the early 1960s.

Good, bad or vile, for a few years the Smiths were cranking out novels at the pace of the pulp magazine writers of the early 20th Century, primarily for publishers who only diehard paperback and adult fiction collectors remember. The confusion is rampant, and online biographies and bibliographies have only complicated matters, codifying completely erroneous attributions of one George H. Smith's novel with the other.[6]

There's the George *Henry* Smith, the man I just referenced, who wrote the Annwn SF novels.

So, who is the *other* George H. Smith?

5   At the time of the original writing in 2010, and at the time of this 2016 publication, the listing was still archived at *http://www.abebooks.com/servlet/BookDetailsPL?bi=154819352&searchurl=an%3D-Smith%252C%2BGeorge%2BH.%26bsi%3D30%26kn%3DIsland%2BSnatchers*. I can also add to this overview of the Annwn series the following, from the George Henry Smith interview from 1993 I acquired after completion of this article: "*The Second War of the Worlds* was part of a series about a Celtic other world named Annwn. *Witchqueen, Kar Kabala, Second War of the Worlds* and *The Island Snatchers* were all set on Annwn. Two other books of the series were *Druid's World* and *Forgotten Planet* which were hardbacks by Avalon. They were also set on Annwn although the editor insisted on *Forgotten Planet* having a different setting. Don

Wollheim bought most of those… when he was at Ace or on his own with DAW…" …" ("An Interview with George H. Smith" by Gary Lovisi, *Paperback Parade* #36, October 1993, pg. 40).

6   For instance, at *http://www.fantasticfiction.co.uk/s/george-h-smith/*

I'm willing to bet a lot of older *Weng's Chop* readers had their introduction to the "poor white bayou trash" sleaze/soap opera genre via Bernard L. Kowalski/Leo Gordon/Gene Corman's hot and steamy **ATTACK OF THE GIANT LEECHES** (1959); that's cuckolded hubby Bruno VeSota fixing his sights on unfaithful swamp-vixen Yvette Vickers (who was the July 1959 *Playboy* centerfold on newsstands just a few months before this movie opened in drive-ins across America)

George *Harmon* Smith was an *über*-prolific writer of sleazy sex novels in the 1950s and '60s, and the man was a machine (on the keyboard; I've no idea what he was like in bed).[7]

It's time to spell out how I do have an emotional stake in all this—if you know my own work in comics, as one of the procession of artists who have delineated the adventures of *Swamp Thing* for DC Comics since the 1970s (my tenure was 1983-1988 or so)—which demands another detour here.

Back in the 1980s, whilst my children were born in our own home and I whittled away at penciling *Saga of the Swamp Thing* from Marty Pasko and Alan Moore scripts damned near every single day, my weekend flea market excursions fed my need for DC Comics back issues featuring characters we were drawing in *Swamp Thing*. Those excursions also exposed me to a curious literary predecessor to our work I had (at the time) no idea existed.

I recall finding my first "swamp hussy" paperback the first summer I was drawing *Swamp Thing*, and since well-worn paperbacks were for the most part still dirt-cheap in flea markets back in those pre-Internet days, I snapped it up immediately.

That planted the seed for what became, over the years, a mounting curiosity about this precursor to our own Abigail Cable, the nominal heroine of *Swamp Thing* since Len Wein and Berni Wrightson launched the title back in the early 1970s, introducing Abigail as Uncle Arcane's Bavarian niece in *Swamp Thing* #2. Arcane became the series villain; Abigail a.k.a. Abby, in time, its heroine.

By the time Abby was in our hands, her Bavarian origins had been essentially forgotten (save for her link with the demonic Arcane), and we made Abby a hard-working, put-upon, blue-collar American heroine all the way.

Well, okay, so she loved an ambulatory spud-man, and had a taste for his hallucinogenic tubers—still, she was pretty likable, I think.

Alan, John, and I definitely made Abby our front-and-center heroine during our tenure on the title. While Abby was hardly "bayou bait" in the grand tradition of the lurid paperbacks and drive-in movies I was drawn to, there's no denying there were roots in those neglected backwaters.

I had grown up catching the occasional bayou-set pot-boiler on late-night television, so I was aware of the pop

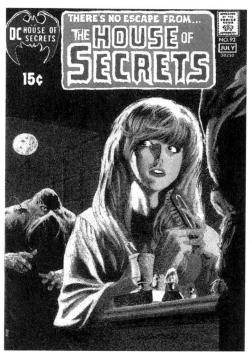

Comicbook author/editor Louise Jones (now Louise "Weezie" Simonson) was the model for Berni (now Bernie) Wrightson's memorable cover for *House of Secrets* #92 (DC Comics, July 1971), which introduced Swamp Thing in a singular, self-standing story scripted by Len Wein, art by Wrightson

cultural archetype. The films I loved above all—monster movies—sported their share of lusty women cheating on their tubby hubbies in brackish bayou country (**ATTACK OF THE GIANT LEECHES**, 1959 comes immediately to mind), but I was increasingly surprised at in-my-hands evidence what had once clearly been a *very* popular paperback genre for lurid so-called "adult" fiction.

In fact, the more of these I stumbled upon, the more I realized the original Len Wein/Berni Wrightson "Swamp Thing" *House of Secrets* #92 (1971) story owed a debt to this peculiar subgenre, populated (as Len's original script was) by real or suspected adultery, homicidally jealous husbands, buxom women, and bodies "buried" in the bayou brine.

Now, *tell me* Len and Berni weren't somehow channeling the gothic ripples of this venerable trash genre. As a genre, it emerged from the literary traditions of William Faulkner, Flannery O'Connor, **TOBACCO ROAD** (1941), **GOD'S LITTLE ACRE** (1958), **NIGHT OF THE HUNTER** (1955), and the like; but it was just as steeped in Cajun superstition and folk tales, steamy swamp-set drive-in cheapies, and the dankest eddies of Southern Gothic lore.

While every comics scholar accurately cites Theodore Sturgeon's short story "It" (first published in *Unknown*,

7   As already noted, since the completion and proofing of this article for final publication in *Weng's Chop*, I have acquired an invaluable 1993 back issue of *Paperback Parade* that provided an excellent overview of the George H. Smiths, the confusion of their credits, and bibliographies for both authors. See "An Interview with George H. Smith" by Gary Lovisi (pp. 29-45), "George H. Smith Paperback Checklist" compiled by Gary Lovisi (pp. 45-55), and especially "Who Were Those Masked Men? The Baffling Identities of George H(enry) Smith and George H(armon) Smith" by James A. Corrick (pp. 56-64), all in *Paperback Parade* #36, October 1993. While I regret not having the opportunity to properly and fully revise this article in the context of my current access to this information, I hasten to add that had I known of (much less owned) this issue of *Paperback Parade*, I likely never would have written this entire essay. Ignorance can be bliss.

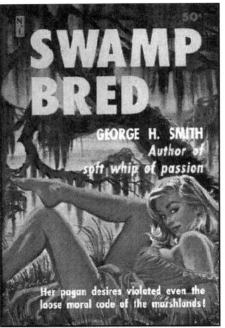

August 1940) as the predecessor for the comicbook swamp monster archetype, the comicbook swampsters also owe a genuine debt to the never-reprinted, forgotten-by-all-but-paperback-collectors "swamp slut" genre—and to its bayou bards, including George *Harmon* Smith.

There's no getting around the fact that these archetypes were known to 1970-era comics creators. The infamous Pre-Code EC Comics beloved by all had included ample bayou-set horror stories in their pages, including the classic "Horror We? How's Bayou?" and the like, and EC's imitators followed suit. Harvey Kurtzman and Will Elder lampooned the clichés of the subgenre in their classic June 1953 *Mad #5* parody "Outer Sanctum" ("Heeeeeeaaap!"). In the 1960s, while the paperbacks we're about to discuss were popping up on newsstands all over the country, rural box-office hits like *Poor White Trash* (the retitled *Bayou*, 1957) and the early black-and-white "roughie" Russ Meyer movies (**LORNA** [1964], **MUD-HONEY** [1965], etc.) further popularized these archetypes.

The underground horror comics that were the immediate contemporaries of the origin stories of *Swamp Thing* and Marvel's *Man-Thing* acknowledged the debt. Richard Corben's very first *Skull* contribution was the rude, crude swamp murder-revenge tale "Lame Lem's Love" (*Skull Comics* #2, 1970), which echoed *very* specific early 1950s Iger Studio/Ajax-Farrell Pre-Code horror comics chestnuts—including stories reprinted in Myron Fass' long-reviled, now celebrated, 1960s and 1970s newsstand black-and-white titles like *Weird* and *Voodoo Tales*—as well as these lurid movies and paperbacks.

It's all visible in Corben's story: an inbred bumpkin husband, a buxom and sexually insatiable wife, adultery, murder, and the return from the grave of said nymphomaniacal bride and her undead beau, exacting final-panel revenge on dumb ol' Lame Lem. These were well-worn clichés juiced by Corben (under his "Gore" *nom de plume*) with more explicit nudity, sex, and violence.

Len and Berni brought another atmospheric, sensitively scripted and illustrated spin to the archetypes, yielding a tragic swamp monster—the titular "Swamp Thing"—along with overwhelmingly positive reader response, a comic book industry "Academy Award", and a spin-off title, *Swamp Thing*, which I found myself penciling under Len's firm editorial hand in 1983.

So, cards on the table: there's my stake in all this.

—

Top: George Harmon Smith's *Swamp Bred* (erroneously listed in some sources as *Swamp Breed*; Newsstand, 1960); George Harmon Smith later wrote young-adult novels including *Bayou Boy* (1965), which won awards and was adapted into a two-part Walt Disney's *Wonderful World of Color* feature (February, 1971, later re-edited/retitled **THE BOY FROM DEADMAN'S BAYOU**). **Above:** splash page to the Pre-Code "Swamp Haunt", from *Haunted Thrills* #5 (January 1953, Ajax-Farrell; writer unknown, art by Joe Doolin).

Who wrote these old paperbacks? Here's a brief overview of a few of the "swamp hussy" titles by George *Harmon* Smith, and others I've stumbled upon over the years since my salad days working on *Saga of the Swamp Thing*…

My odd collection of swamp- and bayou-related original adult paperbacks from the 1950s and 1960s feature titles by one or the other of the notorious George H. Smiths.

My research (and considerable input from Cameron-Wolfe Booksellers in Taos, New Mexico) indicate it's George *Harmon* Smith, not George *Henry* Smith, who scribed a plethora of 1960s "swamp hussy" novels. That is, the George H. Smith who *didn't* write science-fiction erotica, but rather the George H. Smith who wrote tons of brutal, cynical, hard-edged sex novels for Chicago, Illinois-based Novel Books and Newsstand Library.

George *Harmon* Smith wrote a *lot* of these books. The titles are alluring alliterative gems: *Delta Doll, Swamp Bred, Bayou Babe,* and so on.

I've lucked into only a few, but there's more I've since discovered listings and cover images for. *Swamp Bred* is one I'd love to find (*"Her pagan desires violated even the loose moral code of the marshlands!"*). Let's work with what I do have in reach.

From the back cover of *Swamp Lust* (1960, Novel Books):

> *"The second week of their honeymoon, Chad Cain found his wife in bed with another man. He murdered her in a fit of rage, murdered her lover ... but the unique lust inside Claudette could never be killed. It lived on... in Chad's mind... in his loins... in his giant hands...*
>
> *until he saw Claudette in every stacked bosom and long pair of legs that crossed his path... and his life became one constant hunger to recapture Claudette's animal passion... in a thousand other bodies on a thousand successive nights..."*

(Ellipses, natch, are part of the back cover text.)

Swamp Lust was, in many ways, a variation on a number of Pre-Code horror comicbook stories. One in particular comes to mind, "Swamp Haunt", from *Haunted Thrills* #5 (January 1953, Ajax-Farrell; reprinted in Eerie Publications's *Weird* Vol. 1, #12, October 1966 and *Witch's Tales* Vol. 1, #8, September 1969).[8] "Swamp Haunt" and its kind definitely provided the template for Corben's "Lame Lem's Love". *Swamp Lust* was mighty similar, too, though the genders were switched, supplanting "Swamp Haunt"'s male murder victim with a female murder victim, its haunted *femme fatale* with a haunted male murderer. Given the frequency with which Pre-Code horror comics stole material from pulps and radio dramas, they're all likely derived from some earlier pre-1953 short story, novella, or radio play.

In the final chapter of *Swamp Lust*, drunken anti-hero Chad drags a wench named DeWanda into the weeds, hallucinating (as he does throughout most of the novel) that she is his dead wife Claudette. The sex is as rough as the men and women in these trashy novels:

> *"He took her on the loamy earth, mashing her soft body into it. He took her brutally, and that was the way she wanted it, mashing her face into the leaves, arousing*

8   For more on this comic story, including complete scans of the story, see *Myrant*, March 9th, 2011, archived at *http://srbissette.com/?p=11375*

Cover and back cover to George Harmon Smith's infamous *Swamp Lust* (1960, Novel Books); photo cover and uncredited illustration. This scan is of the Novel Book 2nd edition (1962), from the SpiderBaby Archives.

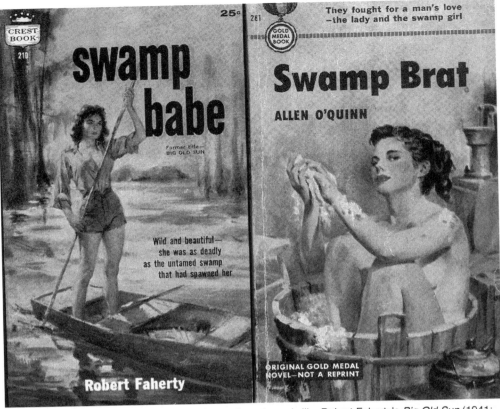

You know it's a genre when the paperback reprints of novels like Robert Faherty's *Big Old Sun* (1941; don't confuse Faherty for documentary filmmaker Robert Flaherty) were published as *Swamp Babe* (March 1958, Crest Books/Fawcett); Allen O'Quinn's *Swamp Brat* (January 1953, Gold Medal Book/Fawcett) was a paperback original from an author who specialized in such steamy southern gothics (consider O'Quinn's subsequent Fawcett novel *A Woman for Henry*, 1954: "Like the swamp she lived in, Morna was a lure and an ending."). This same era was spiced by the failed United Artists feature **BAYOU** (1957) re-edited and re-issued by Cinema Distributors of America as **POOR WHITE TRASH** (1961), becoming a staple of 1960s drive-ins and grind houses.

---

her to the fever pitch... making her buck and rear, like a tormented filly, the first time with the stallion.

'Oh, Chad... you bastard! Oh, Chad... you... sweet, sweet man... don't stop... don't ever stop... I'll kill you if you stop... '"

(Ellipses are from the original text.)

But Chad isn't even *seeing* DeWanda; in his delirium, he only has eyes for one woman:

"It was Claudette.

'Claudette!' he shouted. 'Why have you tortured me like this, you heaven-hell bitch! Why? Why?'

But 'Claudette' didn't hear his drunken, insane shouts; she never heard anything when at the height of her lust. She only writhed beneath him, becoming

one with the hot, passionate ooze of the swamp, her tongue between her teeth.

'I'll stop you from torturing me!' he screamed. Chad was in the throes of his own fulfillment. His hands went to her neck and squeezed the breath out of it. So intent was he as he strangled DeWanda that he never noticed the deadly cottonmouth slithering up to him...

THE END. "

You can see why these novels appealed to me: they're horror stories, almost every one, very much in the idiom (and ripe with the lunacy) of the Pre-Code horror comics they often so resemble—amped up to 1960s adult novel levels.

They are, in their way, naked and revealing sexist tracts. Over 150 pages of *Swamp Lust* spent on a drunken fool like Chad who blames the already-dead Claudette for his *own* procession of crimes and transgressions remains a pretty sobering artifact of 1960s patriarchal projection and madness—Poe, Faulkner, Caldwell, or Flannery O'Connor, it's not, but its relentless *witlessness* comes closer to steeping the reader in the grim, grubby insanity that continues to sire crime in the real world. There's a puritan fusion of shame and shamelessness that's so down-home *American* fueling these crap novels that it's intoxicating. In this, the transparent prose carries its own candor, has its own heat, and brandishes its own shameless integrity in ways more astute and intelligent prose never does.

And the hits kept on coming!

The back cover copy of *Bayou Babe* (June 1960, Novel Books) is as tantalizing as any, which was proudly credited to George H. Smith, "author of *Swamp Lust* and *Delta Doll*" on its title page:

A MOONLIGHT READER

> *"Every man is supposed to have good and bad in him, but this bayou babe brought out the bad so fast and hard that it seemed like the good was just never there at all. She swept into town like a tornado and had every man in it at the breaking point in 24 hours... because she measured 45-24-35 and didn't know the meaning of the word inhibition—COULD ANYONE STOP HER ONE-TRACK BODY?"*

Well, *no.*

Nobody could, and nobody did, though plenty of men try in the novel's sex-and-moonshine-soaked 160 pages.

And it is, of course, all *her* fault.

The novel ends with another sexually frustrated male swigging off his jug and waxing philosophically about his situation...and that he's better off without the *Bayou Babe.*

> *"He took another swig. He was beginning to need a woman again. That last time Lea wanted it so bad and he couldn't give it—that left an ache in him and he wanted to satisfy it real bad right now. 'No damn resolutions are goin' to help, either,' he said, as he got up and started for Mignon's, hopin' to all hell that her husband wasn't home. Even if he is, thought Lucien, I just might throttle him and take her right in front of the old bastard. Yeah, that's just what I very well might do."*

THE END.

Ladies and gentlemen, George *Harmon* Smith!

George Harmon Smith was only one of the many writers that kept this sordid swamp subgenre flowing through the 1950s and 1960s. These aren't "good books," but they *are* entertaining; and they are what they are, and they is what they is, and I'm here to tell you, as one of the *Swamp Thing* creators who labored day and night on that comic, they played a part in what we did, for whatever that's worth. Abby was a wholesome, level-headed woman compared to most of the women in these novels, but still, there are echoes there, in Abby's cut-off jeans and loose tops, in her making her way out to the depths of the swamp to spend time with her swamp man...something

VIOLENCE AND SADISM GRIPPED THE LAND!

Baring their bodies to the lashes of cruel whips, the blood-cultists incited the terrified townspeople to join with them in spreading the mystic scourge over the whole nation. But the young and two-fisted soldier, Malcolm MacAlpine, wielded a slicing sword as he led his troops against the blood maniacs on the loose. And when he wasn't embroiled in seething battle with his enemies, Malcolm satisfied his lust for sex-starved young women, who unhesitatingly yielded to the charms of the brave warrior.

Front and back covers of *Love Cult* (1961, Art Enterprises Inc.), *sans* author credit, which is actually "an exceedingly scarce, possibly pirated edition (or at least made to appear as such)" of George Henry Smith's *Scourge of the Blood Cult* (1961, Epic Books), with "back cover and interior... identical to the Epic edition..." (quoting Richard Cameron-Wolfe's original *abebooks.com* listing).

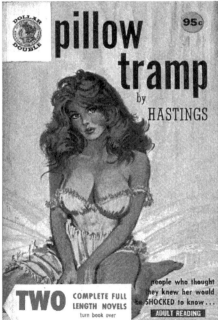

Top: George Henry Smith, as Jerry Jason, authored *Sexodus!* (1963, Boudoir Books), which may have been the novelized expansion of Smith's short story "Fire in the Sky".

Above: In 1962, March Hastings' *Pillow Tramp* was co-published as a "Dollar Double Book" with George Harmon Smith's *Lash of Desire*, most likely a retitled reprint of Smith's *The Whip of Passion* (1959, Newsstand)

to dream about in the wee hours, when the whippoorwills are whipping and the mosquitoes are biting...

—

So: back to it.

George *Henry* Smith vs. George *Harmon* Smith.

Let's see if I can sort this out. And just to complicate matters, yes, *there are pen names involved.*

George *Henry* Smith reportedly wrote novels in a variety of genres under his name and as Jan Hudson.

In the early 1960s, "Jan Hudson" wrote the "Jake Reynolds" sex novels *Love Cult* (1961) and *Love Goddess* (1962, both from Pike Publications), along with a clutch of biker exposés and novels: *The Sex and Savagery of Hell's Angels: The Full Story of America's Motorcycle Wild Ones* (Greenleaf Classics, 1966), *The New Barbarians* (New English Library, 1973), *Bikers at War* (NEL, 1976), etc.

And in these cases, "etc." could mean a *lot* of titles.

There's also a confusion of pseudonyms. George *Harmon* Smith, like George *Henry* Smith, is *also* supposedly the fellow who wrote as Jeremy August, MJ Deer, Robert Hadley, Jan Hudson, Jerry Jason, Dusty North, Hal Stryker, Roy Warren, and so on. Book dealers are attributing both authors to all these pen names, and it's pretty much a clusterfuck.

Let's play the name game.

Jeremy August was credited with *Four Bed Wildcat* (North Hollywood-based Brandon House, 1966) and *Novice Sex Queen* (Brandon House, 1968); MJ Deer is the credited writer of *Flames of Desire, A Place Named Hell* (both from International Publications, 1963); Hadley was the author of *The Velvet Touch* (Midwood Books, 1974).

I'm leaning toward the science-fiction-themed works as being George *Henry* Smith's work: *Space Sex* by "Roy Warren" (from Original Heart, 1965), *Sexodus! The Earth is Doomed* by "Jerry Jason" (Boudoir Limited of Hollywood, CA, 1963), *NYPD 2025* (Pinnacle Books/Crossfire, 1985) by "Hal Stryker", etc., but who knows?

Sexodus! The Earth Is Doomed has a truly tacky cover painting (uncredited) and great cover copy:

> *"...voluptuous women offer their bodies in exchange for life...thrill-happy hordes — without hope of being saved from an exploding sun — fling themselves into one last sensual orgy!"*

But wait, there's more!

Jerry Jason also wrote *The Virgin Agent* (Dominion/TNC Fiction, 1969) and others; my favorite Jerry Jason title is *The Psycho Makers*, (Nite Time Original/Tempo, 1964), with the spicy cover promise:

> *"In Their Diabolical Drive for Power These Hidden Dictators of America Exploited the Seething Sexual Frustration of Weak Willed Men and Women!"*

Vance Packard, move over.

The "Jan Hudson" titles were published by Pike Books, publishers of *The Coming of the Rats*—which I'm pretty sure was by our man, George *Henry* Smith. (More on that next before the wrap-up).

"Jan Hudson" also wrote *Satan's Daughter* (Epic Books/ Art Enterprises, 1961), *Girls Afire* (Imperial Publishing/ Boudoir, 1962), *Hell's Highway* (Pillow Book/Art Enterprises, 1962), *Sorority Sluts* (Epic Books, 1962), *Gang Girls: The Horrible Truth Behind Our Teenage Love Gangs and Their Secret Sex Rites* (Imperial Publishing/ Boudoir Limited Editions, 1963) and *The Dykes: True Stories of Women Who Were Licked But Never Beaten* (Pendulum Books, 1968)—I kid you not, that was the title.

George H. Smith's own name was on some of these, including the evocative title introducing the character St. Germain, *Baroness of Blood* (Pike Books, 1961), and its sequel *Soft Lips on Black Velvet* (Pike Books, 1962), *Strange Harem* (International Publications, 1962), and so on.

Amid this dizzying plethora of titles, I wonder if it's even possible for one writer to have juggled all this—uh, verbiage.

It turns out, one man *didn't*.

According to Cameron-Wolfe Booksellers in Taos, NM, to whom I am enormously indebted for their online information, *some* of this era's adult novels credited to George H. Smith and his various *nom de plumes* in fact "were *not* by science fiction author George H(enry) Smith (who also made forays into this genre), but by George H(armon). [*Note:* George H. Smith books published by Newsstand Library or Novel Books are Harmons, not Henrys.]"

Got that?

The fact is, the George *Henry* Smith books seem to be associated primarily with California and East Coast publishers, hence my emphasis on publishers as I list titles; George *Harmon* Smith's novels are reportedly and uniquely from Novel Books and Newsstand Library, both out of Chicago, IL.

There is a brutal pop poetry to just reading the titles:

George *Harmon* Smith wrote *Dark Desire!* (Newsstand Library, 1959), *Bayou Babe* (Novel Books, 1960), *Female in Heat!* (Novel Books, 1960), *Hot Stuff* (Novel Books, 1960), *Huge Huge Hunger* (Novel Books, 1960; *"He believed that he could take any woman by force and make her glad he had before he was through—and he was right! His name was Lovelady—and he was that for sure—but he was also a perverted sadist—"), Sadist on the Loose!* (Novel Books, 1960), *Swamp Bred* (Newsstand Library, 1960), *Swamp Lust* (Novel Books, 1960), *Brutal Ecstasy* (Novel Books, 1960/1962), *Carnal Cage* (Novel Books, 1962), *Delta Doll* (Novel Books, 1962),

The Golden Hussy (Novel Books, 1962), *Satan's Mate* (Novel Books, 1962), *Shocking She-Animal* (Novel Books, 1962), *Torrid Tramps* (Novel Books, 1962), *Tatan, Titine* (both from Novel Books, 1963), *Lillit* (Novel Books, 1965), etc. – and I do mean *etc.!* I mean, really—*holy shit!*

Check out *Backwoods Hussies* (Novel Books, 1962), which sported an oddly colored cover with the copy:

> *"The raw, realistic story of the constant hunger for new men and new stimulations needed every night by the beautiful women on welfare who have come to be known as the Backwoods Hussies."*

As the folks at Cameron-Wolfe Booksellers note:

> *"The author is clearly critical of the welfare policy of paying women who may have intentionally gotten pregnant out of wedlock. Moralizing Sleaze – what a concept!"*

Get used to it—that was the *modus operandi* of much of this market, the conceit that kept them out of courtrooms much of the time.

Be wary, though, of book dealers claims. *Have pity on them*, trying to sort all this crazy half-century-old fringe publishing shit out.

Pendulum Books house ad for George Henry Smith's (writing as "Jan Hudson") *King of the Teenage Orgies* (1968).

Lottavano per sopravvivere.

RATS

NOTTE DI TERRORE

E non erano soli. Purtroppo.

Top: Albert Neutzel (early *Famous Monsters of Filmland* cover artist) cover art for the first edition of George Henry Smith's *The Coming of the Rats* (November 1961, Pike Books).
Above: Ad art for Bruno Mattei and Claudio Fragasso's feature film **RATS: NIGHT OF TERROR** (*Rats – Notte di Terrore*, 1984)

Some dealers claim George *Henry* Smith wrote books George *Harmon* Smith wrote, including *The Gorgeous Devil* (Newsstand Library, 1959), *Whip of Passion* (Newsstand Library, 1959), and so on. It's a mess, folks.

Hmm, wait a minute. What about the George H. Smith novels from Las Vegas, NV-based Playtime Books?

These include *The Virtuous Harlots* (1963), *Strip Artist* (1964) and *G-String Girls* (1965). Then again, there's also San Diego-based Nightstand Books, publisher of *Leopard Lust* (1967) by "Don Bellmore", who some claim is *another* George H. Smith (but *which one?*) penname.

Or how about the George H. Smith novels for Los Angeles-based Art Enterprises/Moonlight Reader, like *The Year of Love* (1961)?

Or the Dollar Double Book Company two-fers, like *Lash of Desire / Pillow Tramp* (1962, with *Pillow Tramp* credited to "March Hastings")?

Or Softcover Library's *The Lovemakers* (1965)?

The "Jan Hudson" moniker appears on *some* of these, so it looks like George *Henry* Smith's work.

According to the Smith experts at Cameron-Wolfe Booksellers—the one online book dealer who, judging by my own research over the years, seems to have the most accurate take on this Smith conundrum—it was George *Henry* Smith who scribed *Scourge of the Blood Cult*, also published as *Love Cult* (Moonlight Reader, 1961), which would mean the L.A.-based Moonlight Reader imprint was really George *Henry* Smith's publisher.

AAAAAAAAAGGGGGHHHH!!!

—

The biggest conundrum, to my addled mind, is *which* Smith was published by Pike Books?

I suspect those were all from George *Henry* Smith, and those titles include *Private Hell* (1962) along with the couple I've already mentioned.

The one I couldn't sort out for sure—so I tracked down two copies and read the damned thing this summer—is *The Coming of the Rats* (1962), an innovative slice of *"atomic erotica and even post-nuclear porn"*, a sweet turn of phrase from writer Peter D. Smith at his 'blog, Kafka's Mouse.[9]

Horror fiction hounds take note: *The Coming of the Rats* predates James Herbert's rats novels by over a decade. It also predates Stephen Gilbert's *Ratman's Notebooks* (1968, and source for the now-forgotten but enormously popular 1970 genre sleeper **WILLARD**) by a few years.

Is it the work of George *Henry* Smith or George *Harmon* Smith?

---

9   *http://www.petersmith.com/archives/2007/10/08/the-baseball-player-and-the-atom-bomb/*

I'm pretty damned sure this was authored by our man, George *Henry* Smith—and I'll happily stand corrected if someone out there knows better.

Actually, were one to judge a book by its cover(s), *The Coming of the Rats* sounds closer to Bruno Mattei and Claudio Fragasso's Italian movie **RATS: NIGHT OF TERROR** (*Rats – Notte di Terrore*, 1984) than James Herbert's splatterific novels. Here's the back cover copy of the Pike first edition, all caps as they appear on the book itself:

> *"After an Atomic War... WHAT THEN?*
>
> *TODAY a war of H-BOMBS is not only a threatening possibility, but a horrifying reality!*
>
> *TOO FEW of us will survive such a holocaust. TOO FEW of us are PREPARED!*
>
> *But AFTER THE ATOMIC WAR... WHAT THEN?*
>
> *THEN our planet will be populated by whatever LIVING THINGS can best survive the radiation fallout caused by THE BOMBS.*
>
> *AND RATS CAN ABSORB MORE THAN TWICE THE AMOUNT OF RADIATION AS MAN – AND LIVE! IS our planet doomed to be left to the rodents?*
>
> *READ THIS COMPELLING, TERRIFYING NOVEL AND LEARN HOW A POST-ATOMIC WAR ADAM AND EVES* [sic] *BATTLE THE RATS TO THE DEATH!"*

Smith's novel is closer to *End of the World* / **PANIC IN YEAR ZERO!**, right down to the roving rapists who must be dealt with by the novel's nominal hero Steve (you can see why this resonated for me as a lad). The rats only make nominal appearances (including a skirmish with Steve in a looted abandoned grocery store) until the final chapter, a device true to form for George *Henry* Smith, who deferred the arrival of the first Martian cylinders until page 122 of the 174-page *The Second War of the Worlds*. I kid you not!

The bulk of *The Coming of the Rats*, like *The Second War of the Worlds*, involves a not-particularly-likable hero torn between two women, which is why I think it's George *Henry* Smith we're dealing with here.

In *Rats*, our advertising shill (who seems to be the lone man capable of grasping that the End Times are here) is attracted to the lovely, willing, "bang me now" and ready-to-be-Eve-of-the-New-World Mexican lass Rosa, who handily lives with her elder shepherd father *right next door* to Steve's survivalist bomb shelter cave he's busily prepped for life after the Big Ones drop. Steve in fact does make passionate love with Rosa, twice, and oh baby, does she want Steve—Rosa is everything a man could want in the world. But the stupid shithead is smitten with the stunning and spoiled blonde office secretary Bettirose, and to paraphrase the hit tune, *"he just can't get her out of his head"*.

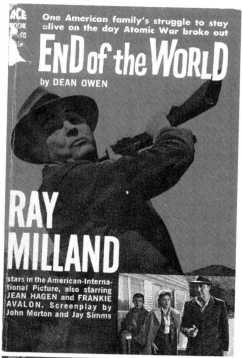

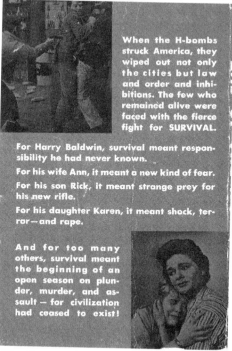

Ultra-Conservative post-apocalyptic machismo fueled Ray Milland/John Morton/Jay Simms' **PANIC IN YEAR ZERO!** (1962), which was novelized and published under its original shooting title *End of the World* (1962, Ace Books)

GEORGE H. SMITH'S
terrifying story of

THE COMING OF THE
RATS

This could
happen
tomorrow!

Cover art by "Michel" for the first UK edition of George Henry Smith's *The Coming of the Rats* (1964, Digit Books, London); scan from SpiderBaby Archives

Bettirose is a brat and a nitwit, but bonedome Steve struggles for *two-thirds* of the novel to get her into his man-cave in the far-enough-from-Ground-Zero-Los-Angeles-to-survive-the-fallout-when-the-bombs-fall hills.

Here's a clue for you how the gender politics go in this 1964 chestnut:

> *"Bettirose had proven to be as useless around a cave as she had been around an office. I had been rebuffed so many times in recent weeks when I had tried to make love to her that she had almost ceased to be a sex object as far as I was concerned."*

Ah, that's a rich vein of 1960s man's man's SF literature. There's nothing quite like it on Earth—well, except maybe the plethora of shit novels from the same fly-by-night publishing houses.

Of course, once the torrent of flesh-eating rats coming pouring out of the hills in the last chapter (pp. 135-158—the final page), Bettirose sees the error of her ways.

Ya see, it takes a *man* facing down a ravenous gray ocean of man-eating mutant rodents to change a damned modern woman's ways in a godforsaken post-apocalyptic world!

It tell you, this is pure unadulterated '60s shit-to-gold alchemy at work, folks![10]

This gem was originally published in 1962 by Van Nuys, CA-based Pike Books. Remember, the earliest George *Henry* Smith novel I know of—*1976: The Year of Terror* (1961)—was published by Los Angeles-based Epic Books, then on Sunset Boulevard, in fact. There's also apparently a link between Epic and Art Enterprises, Inc. of L.A. (the same publisher?), but they're all West Coast imprints.

The Coming of the Rats was subsequently published in the UK in 1964 by Digit/Brown/Watson, and has an edition from Priory Books, too.

To further confuse matters, there's also a highly-collectible version—the second edition?—published by Pike Books under the title *Virgin Mistress* (*"She was a baby-doll with a woman's passion. She wanted to play the game of love but didn't know the rules!"*).

Again, Cameron-Wolfe Booksellers seem to know the inside scoop:

> *"Yet another incarnation of GHS's sci-fi sleaze masterpiece, its new cover and title seeming to promise "goods" (see accompanying scan image) this nevertheless engaging tale cannot (and need not) deliver. The nukes have landed, and the rats are taking over. Humanity's only hope is to fight back while repopulating the earth, via methods involving the courageous coming together of men and women. NOTE: This is the identical page-block as the legendary Pike #203. Even the interior title page gives* The Coming of the Rats. *I suspect that these were leftover page-blocks not bound in the 1961 first print-run. They are cut down in height and width, minimizing the margins. As such, this is ironically the rarest of the four publications of the novel, the remaining two being printed by Digit and Priory."*[11]

---

10 A bit more context: as already noted, new material has been acquired. After completion of this article and while in the proofing stages, bookseller Richard Cameron-Wolfe steered me to the 1993 interview with none other than George *Henry* Smith cited and quoted in earlier footnotes, above. I finally located a copy—too late to properly incorporate its contents into this essay—in which Smith said, "I first got to know Bob Pike when he was an editor for Epic Books. When he started his own publishing house I wrote everything I could for him including books like *The Coming of the Rats* which was based on a short story of mine. I wrote the book in a week or so, so that he could get started. He sometimes came and picked up books at my home in Inglewood because he was on such a tight schedule. He was, I believe, actually an artist or photographer. I lost track of him after I got an agent and started doing other things..." ("An Interview with George H. Smith" by Gary Lovisi, *Paperback Parade #36*, October 1993, pg. 37). I have also recently tracked down a copy of the original adult magazine Smith's *"The Rats"* short story appeared in—which, it turns out, comprises the fateful final chapter of the novel, the only "rat action" in the entire book. At some future date I will prepare a properly revised version of this article reflecting the new information and materials I've uncovered since the completion of this edition for *Weng's Chop*. A writer's and researcher's work is never done, especially when one *thinks* it's done...

11 The listing was up in 2010, and at the time of publication is still at http://www.abebooks.com/servlet/BookDetailsPL?bi=1162984798&searchurl=an%3DSmith%252C%2BGeorge%2BH.%26kn%3DComing%2Bof%2Bthe%2Brats

Advertising the first Pike edition, another dealer (B. Brown & Associates of Seattle, WA) noted, "Albert Neutzel (illustrator). First Edition. 1st ed. Slight wear, Near Fine. An absolute gas of a read, one of the all time great slightly sleazy world catastrophe novels with one of the most famous paperback covers ever done..." (alas, the listing is no longer online).

Albert Neutzel, some of you may recall, also painted some of the early *Famous Monster of Filmland* magazine covers for editor Forrest J. Ackerman and publisher James Warren.

Best of all, good ol' Cameron-Wolfe Booksellers have turned up a retitled edition of Smith's first SF novel, *1976: The Year of Terror*, as *The Year for Love* (!!!):

> *"Exceedingly scarce reprint of Smith's notorious 1976—*The Year of Terror *[Epic # 103]. One of GHS's most original tales, with an excellent mix of science fiction, political intrigue, and sleaze. PLOT: The President has been assassinated, the VP kidnapped, and the US is being terrorized by the Libertarian Party (?!) and the Secret Police. With a supporting cast of spies, hot-rodders, babes, and winos, this thriller is billed as "a sensational story of terror and sadism as ruthless mobs battle the Secret Police in the United States of tomorrow!"..."*[12]

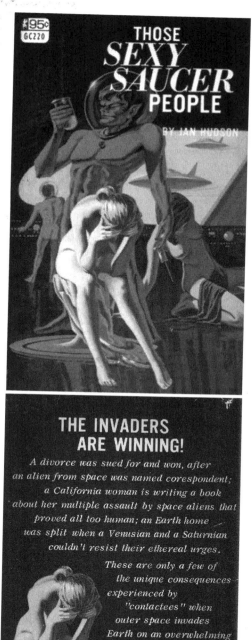

Coolest and rarest of all the George *Henry* Smith sexy SF paperbacks, though—and one I'm overjoyed to have in my collection—is the San Diego-based Greenleaf Classics, Inc. title *Those Sexy Saucer People* (1967). The Greenleaf paperbacks were as lurid and bizarre as any of the '60s. I've had a few in my collection over the years; Ed Wood, Jr.'s novelization of *Orgy of the Dead* (1966) is the most coveted of them all, though the only one I've held on to over the years was the equally rare novelization of Curtis Harrington's delicious *Queen of Blood* (1966), with a fantastic Albert Neutzel painted cover.

Those Sexy Saucer People was Smith's lurid account of supposedly real-life sexual "close encounters" with aliens. For the most part, it's a typical 1960s UFO investigation text, with relatively little sexual content—but oh, that cover! The promise of explicit extraterrestrial sexual antics promises all the sizzle. Dig the back cover copy:

> *"The invaders are winning! A divorce was sued for and won after an alien from space was named correspondent; a California woman is writing a book about her multiple assault by space aliens that proved all too human; an Earth home was split when a Venusian and a Saturnian couldn't resist their ethereal urges."*

Oh, yes, the martians *are* coming.

Second War of the Worlds, indeed:

The Tripods fall; the Towers rise...

---

12 The 2010 listing was still online at the time of publication, at *http://www.abebooks.com/servlet/BookDetailsPL?bi=1314792706&-searchurl=sts%3Dt%26tn%3D1976%2BYear%2Bof%2BTer-ror%26x%3D6%26y%3D14*

Previous page: Front and back cover (art by Ed Smith), *Those Sexy Saucer People* by George Henry Smith as "Jan Hudson" (1967, Greenleaf Classics). **Above:** Original United Artists ad campaign for the swamp-lust exploitation film **BAYOU** (1957). **Below:** Front and back cover (design and penciled by Roger Dean, painted by Tim White), *War of the Worlds: Global Dispatches*, edited by Kevin J. Anderson (June 1996, Bantam Books). **Following page:** Abby and Swamp Thing commission art © John Totleben (2005)

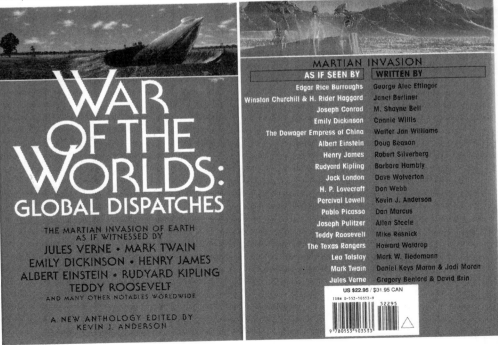

"Holmes vs. Red Planet Mars Redux II Or; Who is George H. Smith, Really?" September 18, 2010, http://srbissette.com/?p=9639
"Swamp Hussies & Bayou Babes! The Secret Origins of Abby Cable & Sordid Confessions of a Swamp Thing Artist," March 8, 2011, http:// srbissette.com/?p=11344
"Holmes vs. Red Planet Mars Redux III Or; Swamp Sluts, Rodent Ram- pages, and Oh Those Sexy Saucer People!" September 20, 2010, http:// srbissette.com/?p=9659

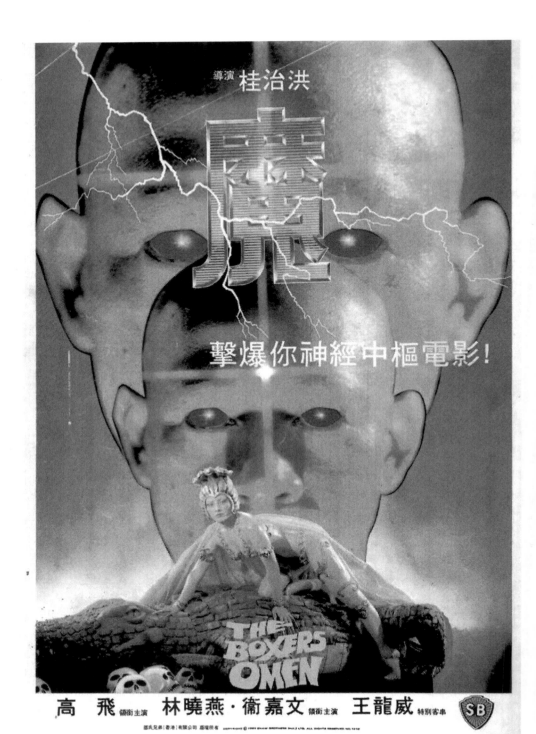

Original theatrical poster for **THE BOXER'S OMEN**

TUESDAY NIGHT GRINDHOUSE NIGHTS AT THE NEW BEVERLY:
SHAWTEMBER

Starring Bennie Woodell!

*The month of September was redubbed "Shawtember" at the New Beverly Cinema. All month long films from the Shaw Brothers were screened; a few were rare prints and other newly made 35mm prints from Celestial Pictures. Not only were the Shaw Brothers celebrated during their Tuesday Grindhouse Night programming, but also every Wednesday/Thursday program and their Saturday midnight movies were Shaw films, on top of some kiddie matinees, like **SUPER INFRAMAN** (Zhong guo chao ren, a.k.a. **INFRA-MAN**, 1975). It was a wonderful month to be in Los Angeles, to see films like **KING BOXER** (Tian xia di quan, a.k.a. **FIVE FINGERS OF DEATH**, 1972), **THE MASKED AVENGERS** (Cha shou, 1981), **THE MIGHTY PEKING MAN** (Xin xing wang, a.k.a. **GOLIATHON**, 1977)[1], and **CHINESE SUPER NINJAS** (Ren zhe wu di, a.k.a. **FIVE ELEMENT NINJAS**, 1982) all in glorious 35mm, but they saved the real fun and some of the real obscure flicks for Tuesday nights.*

September 15th, 2015

I saw two Shaw Brothers horror flicks being screened: **BLACK MAGIC** (*Jiang tou*, 1975), which I had never seen before, and **THE BOXER'S OMEN** (*Mo*, 1983). Now the fun part of this night—that truly gave us the Grindhouse experience—was the theater being down to one projector instead of two...they couldn't get it fixed in time. So after every reel, the lights came up, the screen went black and we had a two-minute intermission as they put on the next reel. It just felt right for some reason.

There were two Hong Kong horror trailers screened before **BLACK MAGIC**, both of which were for films I have never heard of before: **RETURN OF THE DEMON** (*Mo gao yi zhang*, 1987) and **DEAD CURSE** (*Meng gui po ren*, 1985). Both of these looked like a wild good time, and **RETURN OF THE DEMON** even had a werewolf! They were your typical late-'80s Hong Kong horror films that mixed action and comedy in with the scares.

BLACK MAGIC was the first film up for the night, and from what they said before the screening, the film was the very first Shaw Brothers horror film, and that it was very tame compared to where they went later on in the studio's horror filmography. I had a lot of fun watching movie, but it truly was very tame and not really that scary...but it had so many great things going for it. The basic plot: there's a witch doctor (Ku Feng) who can put a love spell on someone if you get their hair and blood, so this woman (Ni Tien) tries this on Xu Nuo (Ti Lung), who's marrying another woman. He is taken by her spell, but then the witch doctor puts the spell on the woman for

Original theatrical poster for **BLACK MAGIC**

his own gain. The story really isn't much to write home about, but the crowd had quite a number of laugh-out-loud moments, including early on in the film where the witch doctor was milking a woman for a potion. It was incredibly random, but we all loved it. And surprisingly, being such an early horror film, the special effects were quite good, even grossing me out in a scene that involved

1 See *Weng's Chop* #6, p.11

worms. That's all I'm going to say. I would definitely seek out **BLACK MAGIC** if you have a chance!

The second film for the night was **THE BOXER'S OMEN**. This film I saw many, many years ago. I forgot most of what happened in it, I just knew it was crazy, so I was ready to see it again. Because of the projector issue, there were no trailers before this film; we were already running very late into the evening as it was.

But when I said I forgot most of what happened in the film, halfway through watching it I realized I hadn't forgotten what the film was about; I just plain downright never knew what the hell was going on the first viewing… and I sure as hell didn't understand the second viewing! I don't think anyone really did, quite honestly; people were looking at each other laughing for a good portion of the movie, and laughing during our two-minute intermissions about what we just went through. All I could decipher was something about a boxer who wronged the triads, and Bolo Yeung was trying to kill him. It was great seeing Yeung in the film; he always plays the perfect villain. But where this movie fails on plot (well, maybe things are lost in translation…I'm going to at least give it the benefit of the doubt), the film exceeds in craziness and grossing-out. There's a Buddhist monk birthing a bat from an old woman's mouth, then sacrificing it to a Bat Man who comes and resurrects it; there's a weird green alien coming from a bloody pulp to fight the monk; there's alligator sex and killing an alligator to gut it and put a body inside to rebirth it. There's plenty more crazy stuff that happens in the film…you really have to see it to fully appreciate the insanity of **THE BOXER'S OMEN**!

September 22nd, 2015

The projector was back up and running and we had an even crazier double-feature, starting with **BAMBOO HOUSE OF DOLLS** (*Nu ji zhong ying*, 1973), a Shaw Brothers women-in-prison (WIP) film. Before that screened, there were three trailers shown, all of them being WIP films, they were **99 WOMEN** (*Der heiße Tod*, 1969)[2], **REFORM SCHOOL GIRLS** (1986), and another Hong Kong WIP film from the late '80s that never showed an English title, just the Chinese title. It looked good, but I'll never know what it was called. **99 WOMEN** looked fun, but **REFORM SCHOOL GIRLS** really had the crowd going. I think the New Beverly, if they can find a print of it, should screen that one night. From the reaction the crowd was giving, it'd be a great screening.

I had never seen **BAMBOO HOUSE OF DOLLS** before, and I wasn't quite sure how far the Shaw Brothers

2   See *WC #6*, p.38

Left Top to Bottom: One of the best and most insane Chinese supernatural horror films every made, **THE BOXER'S OMEN** builds to its nightmarish climax utilizing regional and fictional folklore and black magic to achieve its goal. Gore and goo and bug-eyed monsters populate this classic. Where the heck is the Blu-ray, Criterion?

would be able to go in a WIP film, but I learned quite fast that they could go as far as they wanted! The first half-hour was pretty much nothing but lots of nudity (full nudity), girls fighting each other, different forms of humiliation (like the girl cleaning the floors being forced to lick the boots of the woman in charge), etc. Though it was a lot of fun, I was wondering if and when there'd be a story to somewhat follow, which at about thirty minutes in, there was. It involves a secret agent who poses as a female prisoner going into the prison to find someone on the inside who knows where some gold is stashed, and to have his help in retrieving it, but the people in charge of the prison also know of this gold and are on alert for anyone trying to escape to find it. There were a lot of intense sequences that kept me on the edge of my seat once the film started going. I think the first time the girls try to break out of the prison is one of the better prison breakout sequences I've seen. It was a good ten, fifteen minutes and it was paced perfectly! Even though the second jailbreak wasn't as intense with regards to "Are they going to get caught?", it was "Damn, this is a lot of fun because they're not holding back!" The film is also filled with spies and double-crossings, and a final action sequence that made the film more memorable than it already was. For a film that started out as pure sleaze, **BAMBOO HOUSE OF DOLLS** really turned around into a really good, solid film that I would definitely like to be a part of my collection.

The second film in the double feature was **HUMAN LANTERNS** (*Ren pi deng long*, 1982), one of the Shaw Brothers' great horror films! The trailers beforehand were from the week prior that we were supposed to see before **THE BOXER'S OMEN** that just got scrapped because of the projector issue. They were **BLOOD RITUAL** (*Xie luo ji*, 1989)[3] and **BRUTAL SORCERY** (*Du gu*, 1983), two more Hong Kong horror films that

Original theatrical poster for **BAMBOO HOUSE OF DOLLS**

seemed like a good time, but I've never heard of them and don't know if they're even available anywhere.[4]

HUMAN LANTERNS, though, is a damn good film. Kind of like **THE BOXER'S OMEN** in the sense where I kind of knew what was going on, but a lot of was happening that might have been lost in translation. Chao Chun-Fang (Lo Lieh) makes lanterns and he's commis-

4   Though they don't have any official domestic releases, they can be found through various "grey area" sources by those capable of a little diligent Googling. –*ed.*

HUMAN LANTERNS

of it was. It was amazing to watch—I mean, who doesn't want to see Chen Kuan Tai and Lo Meng fighting; they were two of the Shaw's best—but it just seemed really out of place, or like they were filling an action quota of some sort. But there were some amazing horror elements and atmosphere. Chun-Fang's lair seemed like an old Universal monster film set or something of that sort... it was creepy as all hell, and the perfect place to tie up women, slice open the top of their heads, and pour mercury into the slit to make it easier to tear off the skin. The special effects were fantastic in this film. I was grossed out beyond belief when we see Lieh actually tearing the skin off of the girls and then holding it up. It looked real! And the women really sold the fear and pain they were in, the acting was more solid than most horror films I've seen. Finally, I loved Chun-Fang's costume. He was like an orangutan but with a skeleton face, and the acrobatics that he was performing while trying to capture the women were just as good as anything you'd see in a Venom Mob film. **HUMAN LANTERNS** is a must-see for any Shaw Brothers or horror fan.

September 29th, 2015

Before the first film, **THE AVENGING EAGLE** (*Leng xue shi san ying*, 1978), there was a Warner Brothers cartoon titled *Ready, Woolen, and Able* (1960), which pitted a giant sheep dog against a wolf (that looked like Wiley Coyote only with a red nose to differentiate the two). The wolf tried to get the sheep, the dog stopped him. It was a lot of fun and got lots of laughs from the audience. I love it when they show the old cartoons at the New Beverly.

After the cartoon, we were shown a trailer reel of films that were coming to the New Beverly the first week of October which included **THE HILLS HAVE EYES** 2006 remake and its 2007 sequel, **THE EXORCIST** (1973), which will be screening at midnight a few Saturdays in October, and the original trailer for **ALIEN** (1979).

In **THE AVENGING EAGLE**, Chi Ming-sing (Ti Lung) is being hunted by a few men. He meets Cheuk Yi-fan (Fu Sheng), who helps him and decides to continue with him on his journey for revenge against the 12 other Eagles from Ming-sing's clan. The film's plot can get convoluted at times because a good portion of it is told in flashbacks, which is something I love, but they stay on the flashback so long that you forget that what you're watching isn't actually the present and when they go back to Yi-fan and Ming-sing you're like, "Oh, yeah, that's right, I forgot about Yi-fan." But the one thing this film has going for it acting-wise is the rapport between Ti Lung and Fu Sheng. They both act off each other so well, and they're both probably the best actors in the Shaw Brothers stable. Aside from the plot and acting, this film has a ton of action in it, and all of it is top-notch kung fu that makes you craving more! Each of the 13 Eagles has their own weapon, one of which uses the golden ring! You would think a giant ring versus a sword would end with the sword winning, but it's always mind-blowing how someone can defend and attack with a ring and de-

sioned by someone of importance to make one that will win a contest. Chun-Fang then kidnaps women to skin them alive and make lanterns out of them. It seems pretty obvious what the film is about, but there is so much swordplay happening from Chen Kuan Tai and Lo Meng that I was completely lost with regards to what the point

Insane kung fu explodes in **FIVE DEADLY VENOMS**

feat all their opponents. It's those weapons that I love watching in kung fu films. Swords are fun and all, but everyone uses a sword; give me a guy who uses a ring or a half tambourine made out of spikes! And of course what would a film called **THE AVENGING EAGLE** be without showcasing the Eagle style of kung fu? Luckily for us, they took it one step further and had the head Eagle wear gold plated, sharp-as-hell talons on his hands to make every strike a potentially deadly one! Definitely check out **THE AVENGING EAGLE**—it's actually streaming on Netflix right now—you won't regret it!

The second film of the night was the **FIVE DEADLY VENOMS** (*Wu du*, 1978), one of the most famous, quintessential kung fu films ever. Before the film, however, we saw three trailers: **STREET GANGS OF HONG KONG** (*Fen nu qing nian*, 1973), **FEARLESS FIGHTERS** (*Tou tiao hao han*, 1971), and **FIVE FINGERS OF DEATH** (*Tian xia di yi quan*, 1972). I had never heard of the first two, but they didn't look anything exceptional,

but **FIVE FINGERS OF DEATH** is a classic, for sure. There's not too much to add to things that have already been said about the **FIVE DEADLY VENOMS**. It's one of the few Shaw Brothers films that have way more plot and story than action, but it's told in such a good way with mystery and deception that you can't help but not get engrossed in the film. And then when there is action, you're treated to quite possibly the greatest martial arts team that has ever been put together. The Venom Mob was special, and there's a reason they made countless films together. What makes the action so great, though, is that we're treated to animal styles that aren't really shown otherwise. Everyone knows the snake style, but not many people know of the centipede or toad styles of kung fu, so to see them on-screen is a joy. Anyone reading this has probably already seen this film, but if you haven't, put down this magazine right now, go get a copy of the film and prepare to see one of the best Shaw Brothers films of all time!

WHY SHOULD I RECEIVE A PRIZE? I KNOW THAT I'M A GENIUS!

COMING IN 2016

from Wildside/Kronos Productions

THE BARN: BRINGING THE FUN BACK TO HORROR

An Interview with Director Justin M. Seaman

by Steven M. Ronquillo

There have been many movies that try to be '80s throwbacks following grindhouse traditions, however, all but a chosen few have been such slaves to a look that they forget the big reason we watch movies like **THE MUTILATOR** *(1984) or* **NEON MANIACS** *(1986)...FUN! At the Monster-rama drive-in fest at Vandergrift, PA, I met Justin Seaman and his crew promoting and showing the trailer to* **THE BARN** *(2016), and I was taken aback by what looks to be a fun movie about three unique killers returning each Halloween, if you're dumb-ass enough to knock on the barn door (thank God we had a lot of them back then), and their mission is to kill some folks so the devil can have his supper. If that alone brings a big-ass cheesy grin to your mug, this is the movie for you. If not, then get the hell on while we all enjoy it!*

Weng's Chop had a chance to sit down with the director and some others to talk about this fun little gem with an awesome soundtrack...so we took it.

Tell our readers about yourself, and how you got your start in filmmaking.

My name is Justin M. Seaman, and other than being cursed with a terrible last name best suited for a shipmate or a job in the adult entertainment industry (*cough*), I'm an aspiring filmmaker. I started making home movies when I was about five years old with the family camcorder, and that led to a lot of my friends hanging out and making short films through high school and eventually into college, where we formed Nevermore Production Films near Pittsburgh, PA.

What are your favorite '80s films, and did they influence your movies?

Some of my favorites are **NIGHT OF THE DEMONS** [1988], **DEMONS** [*Dèmoni*, 1985], **A NIGHTMARE ON ELM STREET** [1984], **NIGHT OF THE CREEPS** [1986], **TRICK OR TREAT** [1986][1] and **THE MONSTER SQUAD** [1987]. Yes, they highly influenced me as a director, and my film **THE BARN**. I put many homages to those movies into my latest film.

Since this is, as you call it, "a love note to the '80s", what about the '80s do you love?

I love the music, the hair, the outfits, and just the overall style of filmmaking that was being done in the '80s. The one-sheets and box art that came out of that time period are also amazing and that is exactly what I am trying to recreate with **THE BARN**.

---

1   See *Weng's Chop* #4.5, p.100

How did you come up with the idea for the plot?

I spent most of my summers at my grandparents' house in the country. There wasn't much to do other than watch TV or play outside. So needless to say I found myself struggling to keep entertained. One day I noticed an old barn far off in the distance, and thought to myself "I wonder what's in there…maybe monsters?" That's when the story came to life. I wrote a small book soon after that became the backbone to the screenplay 20 years later.

Whats it like being part of the historic Pittsburgh film scene?

It is great being able to say our film was made in the zombie capital of the world.

Who are the three killers, and were they movie-inspired?

They are The Boogeyman, Hallowed Jack , and The Candycoorn Scarecrow. Not really movie-inspired per se, but lots of fans tend to think they were inspired from other baddies such as Freddy Krueger, Harry Warden, and **DARK NIGHT OF THE SCARECROW** [1981][2] to name a few. Honestly it's been so long that it's hard to remember the exact reasoning to why I chose these creatures.

How did you create the backstory behind the killers?

It was really about the Devil wanting to eat the flesh of the living and that he had servants that could walk among the living to do his dirty work on Halloween. So I started thinking about what kind of creatures would be on a farm and how would they disguise themselves…so I ended up with a miner, a pumpkin man and a scarecrow.

Have you submitted the film to the festival circuit yet?

We have not submitted it to any film festivals yet, but plan to in the future.

What do you want the fans to get out of your movie?

Well, most importantly I want to make it clear that I am not trying to make a film that is necessarily going to scare you. The horror audience has become desensitized over the years, and what scares one person might not scare

nine others. So I set out to make a fun, entertaining flick. A film that once the viewing is over, you are smiling because you had a blast watching the movie.

Will you make further films?

Hopefully, as the long as the first one sells.

How did you get the amazing score?

Rocky Gray contacted me after seeing the one-sheet released on *Fangoria.com* and he thought it was amazing. So we got to talking, and he really wanted to be a part of the project. Now the soundtrack will be available from Lunaris Records.

Out of all the cool rewards you are giving away as perks, which ones are going to be sold after the Indiegogo campaign ends?

As of right now the only items that will be available after the Indiegogo campaign will be the t-shirts, board game, CD soundtrack, *The Barn The Video Game* download, and qoster. Currently we are now InDemand on Indiegogo, which means that people can continue to get what's left of our perks for a short time period, including pre-ordering the DVD. (*http://igg.me/at/TheBarnMovie*)

I notice your companies name is Nevermore Production Films—is that a reference to The Raven?

Yes it is Poe-inspired. Fun Fact: If you watch closely in the film you will see that line from *The Raven* written on a chalkboard in the schoolhouse scene.

Thank you for your time. Justin. Any more info for our readers?

Thanks for having me. Check out our Facebook page at *facebook.com/TheBarnmovie* and our website *nevermoreproductionfilms.com* for all the latest news on the film.

—

AFTERWARD: **THE BARN** had its world premiere at the Hollywood Theater in Dormont, PA on Halloween weekend, and sold out both showings.

2 See *WC #6.5*, p.104

More Golden Age Porn for the Connoisseur

by Louis Paul

The restoration of films from our past has been hoped for and anticipated by cinephiles for a variety of reasons. For years, the restoration (and eventual release onto VHS, and later, DVD and Blu-ray) of films by the likes of David Lean and a number of the movies in the Alfred Hitchcock library took precedence over fan favorite genre films.

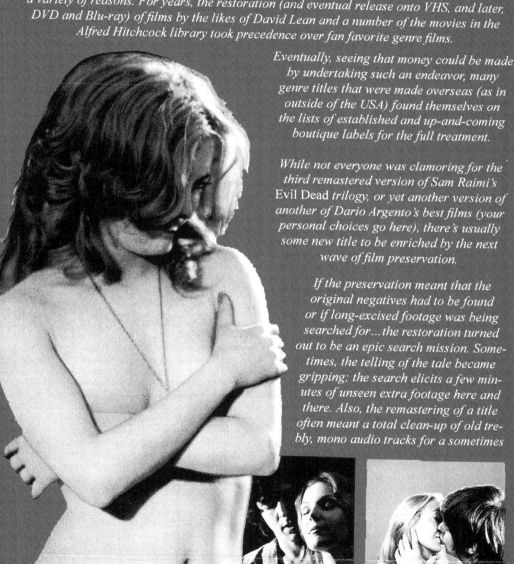

Eventually, seeing that money could be made by undertaking such an endeavor, many genre titles that were made overseas (as in outside of the USA) found themselves on the lists of established and up-and-coming boutique labels for the full treatment.

While not everyone was clamoring for the third remastered version of Sam Raimi's Evil Dead *trilogy, or yet another version of another of Dario Argento's best films (your personal choices go here), there's usually some new title to be enriched by the next wave of film preservation.*

If the preservation meant that the original negatives had to be found or if long-excised footage was being searched for…the restoration turned out to be an epic search mission. Sometimes, the telling of the tale became gripping; the search elicits a few minutes of unseen extra footage here and there. Also, the remastering of a title often meant a total clean-up of old trebly, mono audio tracks for a sometimes sterling solid job, pumping up flat and tinny mono sound to full-fledged wall-shaking stereo and beyond (does anyone remember the furniture shaking effects of THX audio?).

While there's the usual suspects of directors in the horror genre particularly who have had their movies released in less-than-ideal versions both on the screen and even on VHS, and DVD (even some Blu-ray releases could have been more improved considering the technology) that leaves one to wonder (well, at least I did)...what about all that classic smut from the 'Seventies and 'Eighties?

The late Mike Vraney (of Something Weird Video) rescued hundreds, if not thousands of obscure titles from the strangest places, and released these movies onto VHS first, and then DVD. While for the most part, the majority of these films were straight telecine transfers from 16mm and 35mm original negatives and prints, every now and then "star" genre directors (like H.G. Lewis, for example) got their movies remastered as best as can be considering the original source elements that the labs had to work with.

In the case of hundreds of X-rated titles from the very dawn of Porn's golden age, SWV just transferred them straight...much like the movies themselves, warts and all. The splicey, color- faded, or all-purple and -red prints with bad hollow sound (many of the more obscure titles were shot in one or two days, hence the absence of elaborate camera set-ups and careful audio recording) found themselves in-demand by adult cinema aficionados and bad cinema enthusiasts everywhere. That they even exist today is part of the charm.

In recent years, video companies such as Alpha Blue, Caballero, Alternative Images, and After Hours Cinema have made varied attempts at restoring adult movies to their former colorful if seedy glory, but none have really come close as recent triumphs from Distribpix and Vinegar Syndrome, two small companies that invested in remastering some of the better, some of the more obscure, as well as some of the more notorious titles the genre has to offer. I'm still trying to figure out why Vinegar Syndrome is so keen on the titles of one Carlos Tobalina, a filmmaker who displayed average talent as a director (in most cases), and undoubtedly Ed Wood-ian ineptitude in others; Tobalina also photographed, cast, and scored the music for the majority of movies he directed. He made a two-hour plus epic (**MARILYN AND THE SENATOR** [1975]) about prostitution and a potential Watergate-like scandal and filmed nearly fifty more titles in his seventeen-year career. With our little primer on film restoration done, let's jump right to the movies.

French DVD company Arte Video's release of Joe Sarno's 1975 classic

nifer Jordan performing as Sarah Nicholson) who left her small fishing village in disgrace, and returns to find there's no warm welcome for her. As before, the women of the town resent her, mostly because their husbands want to fuck her, and she just wants to teach them that free love is the only way to live...forever and ever.

Oddly enough, as the movie unfolds Abigail appears to not be the main character as much as she is a catalyst for the events that happen in this Long Island town (actually, Amityville, Long Island [yes, *that* Amityville], site of one of director Joe Sarno's homes in the 'Seventies).

Before leaving for points unknown, she was caught screwing with the married husband (an uncharacteristically subdued Jamie Gillis) of one of her friends (Mary Mendum/Rebecca Brooke). Their marriage shattered, the wife has been carrying on an affair with a local out-of-work fisherman (Eric Edwards)...enter the returning Abigail, who seeks to wreak havoc with everyone's lives, and get her own skyrocketing libido satisfied as well.

ABIGAIL LESLEY
IS BACK IN TOWN

1975, USA. D: Joe Sarno

S: *Jennifer Jordan (a.k.a. Sarah Nicholson), Mary Mendum (a.k.a. Rebecca Brooke), Eric Edwards, Jamie Gillis, Jennifer Welles, Chris Jordan*

This well-regarded movie is a moralistic tale about a woman on the cusp of middle-age named Abigail (Jen-

The early 'Seventies was a goldmine for the best of the Golden Age porn films. For some audiences, those movies that were a little less sexually explicit but still got across the same vibe were preferable. Today, we refer to those films as softcore. The late Joe Sarno (1921-2010) was, and is still, considered by many to be a master sexploitation filmmaker.

Sarno's style was unusual (even by the standards of the genre in which he worked). He preferred to write his own scripts, which essentially were moralistic dramas with the emphasis on sex. Sarno always planned out his sex pictures as actual movies first, and then as a source of titillation second. He is quoted as saying he'd rather photograph the face of a woman enduring an orgasm, which reveals so much more... than do a close-up of her moist, wet vagina leaking love juices. Those are not his words exactly, but gets across his point across in the most direct manner.

While he often sidestepped working in hardcore films in his early years (both he and his wife Peggy claimed in the excellent documentary A LIFE IN DIRTY MOVIES [2013] that he did not make hardcore features until after '73) there is proof that, to the contrary, even in his adopted second home country of Sweden (although he was born in Brooklyn, New York), he was making hardcore features as well as softer versions of the same movies as early as 1970. For Sarno the filmmaker, the most unique and cleverest way to show the multi-faceted emotions of two people having sex (real or otherwise) was to get his camera (he was often his own DP on many of his movies) up close to their faces and their upper bodies. He claimed he wasn't interested in the gynecological close-ups that became a mainstay of the genre, and yet, some of his sex films (the Swedish FABODJANTAN [1978] and the made-in-the-USA films INSIDE JENNIFER WELLES [1974], TIGRESSES...AND OTHER MAN-EAT-ERS [1977], and DEEP INSIDE ANNIE SPRINKLE [1981]) contain some of the more outré and transgressive sexual scenes outside of seedier films from the likes of the Avon company.

ABIGAIL LESLEY IS BACK IN TOWN was intended to cash-in on the then-popular craze for hardcore films that couples could go see in a movie theater utilizing a better-than-average cast of performers who were active in the adult movie genre (Edwards, Gillis, Welles), and two relative newcomers (Mendum and Jordan, who beforehand appeared in stage plays and musicals, before adopting a variety of aliases and finding their way through a few softcore flicks before entering the hardcore genre). Mendum, more popularly known via her Rebecca Brooke pseudonym, had already appeared in the very hot French hardcore feature FELICIA (1975) for the director Max Pecas, and that film gained some notoriety for its scorching lesbian scenes with (young-appearing, but of legal age) co-star Beatrice Harnois. In this movie, Mendum/Brooke and co-star Jean Roche (as her husband) take their neighbor's playful daughter on an exotic holiday, unaware that she will shortly explode their libidos through the roof and leave her fellow cast members—as well as the viewers—drained. Oddly enough, many people recall this movie as a titillating softcore feature, unaware of its original version. I recall seeing an uncut English-dubbed XXX print in the late 'Seventies in a Times Square porno theater, but that version has never resurfaced either on VHS or DVD in this country since. Regardless, the original version, in French, under the title LES MILLE ET UN PERVERSIONS DE FELICIA is uncut, and worth seeking if you can find it on the Internet.

Lastly, I'd like to see the hardcore version of ABIGAIL LESLEY IS BACK IN TOWN that I saw in Times

Jennifer Jordan and Mary Mendum have a scintillating tryst in this scene from
ABIGAIL LESLEY IS BACK IN TOWN

LAURA'S TOYS

1975, Sweden/USA. D: Joe Sarno

S: Mary Mendum (Rebecca Brooke), Eric Edwards, Katja von Graff, Anita Eriksson

A deliciously madcap sex movie, the likes they don't make anymore, **LAURA'S TOYS** stars Eric Edwards as an archeologist named Walter, who with his wife, Laura (Mendum/Brooke) are excavating the seaside areas of Sweden for some fabled archeological find. The always handsome but perpetually frustrated husband (Laura appears sexually inhibited but is anything but) soon starts bedding the duo's personal assistant Anna (comely Swedish lass Graff). Planning revenge because her no doubt steamy hairy bush is beginning to turn into a water sprinkler of passion, Laura rekindles her passionate girl-on-girl romance with Hanni (Eriksson) and together the two plan on first filling Anna's ears with tales of Laura and Hanni's first lesbian experiences back in school when they were teenagers, and then more ribald tales of Sapphic lust. Eventually, Anna is left all panting and wet and would rather fall under the seductive powers of this pair rather than continue swallowing Edwards' man meat. Needless to say, he becomes more frustrated.

Is it as good a film as **ABIGAIL LESLEY**? No, not really, in my opinion. As much as they are similar in that primary cast members are shared, and both take place near water, **LAURA'S TOYS** is much more concerned with the Sapphic love angle, which oddly addresses the "revenge" angle as a mere excuse to show us more titillating lips-on-furry-thigh love-fests. I've never seen a graphic XXX-rated version of this film, but I would not hedge my bets saying one does not (or at the least, did not) exist.

Retro-Seduction Cinema's DVD double bill of **ABIGAIL LESLEY** and **LAURA'S TOYS** is fine indeed. While the picture quality is pleasing at best, if occasionally soft in spots, there are many extras including an audio commentary which includes Sarno himself, self-proclaimed biographer Michael Bowen, and Michael Raso, president of the video company that released the disc. Other extras include a short interview with Peggy Sarno about shooting **ABIGAIL** in Amityville, Long Island, and her and Joe working with hardcore actors. One has to take some things that Peggy says in the interview with a grain of salt, as she states that Joe rarely made hardcore films and yet it is well known that he made several before shooting this duo. Another item of interest is that in the aforementioned documentary **A LIFE IN DIRTY MOVIES**, Peggy pretty much plays coy about being an actress in Joe's movies, as suddenly the screen is filled with B&W footage of her frolicking naked as the pseudonymously named leading actress in a number of Joe's movies. Other extras on the RS Cinema disc include a batch of Sarno trailers (The crazy **YOUNG PLAYTHINGS** [1972] among them), more commentaries, and for **LAURA'S TOYS** there's even an interesting Eric Edwards audio commentary where he mentions other highlights from his career.

1975, SWEDEN/USA. D: JOE SARNO
AVAILABLE FROM RETRO SEDUCTION CINEMA

Production shot of Joe Sarno (left) on the set of
LAURA'S TOYS in 1975

Square back in the day. While I'm not aware if Sarno filmed the XXX-rated footage himself or not, it certainly looked organic enough that it appeared that it was far from inserts. It also made the movie appear more sensual and natural. I think, more than likely, Sarno's producers or distributors were hoping to recoup some of their investment and the movie just wasn't cutting it as a softcore feature at a time when hardcore was all the rage. Now, I would hazard to guess that Sarno shot this film both ways, and eventually was forced to use the hardcore footage for one of the releases. This disc could have used both versions, but I understand that Peggy Sarno (as well as Joe before his death) claimed that he envisioned this and shot it without graphic, pornographic footage. Being that it is highly regarded as one of his best films, I can understand why they toe this line, but seeing as how directly before and afterwards he worked strictly making adult films (using a variety of aliases), I think the odds are high that one day we'll see this version turn up.

1975, USA. D: JOE SARNO
AVAILABLE FROM RETRO SEDUCTION CINEMA

LAURA'S TOYS

A scene from Joe Sarno's **LAURA'S TOYS** ...breaking the barriers of X and XXX erotica

BARBARA BROADCAST

1977, USA. D: Henry Paris (a.k.a. Radley Metzger)

S: Annette Haven, Jamie Gillis, C.J. Laing, Susan Mc-Bain, Constance Money, Wade Nichols, Sharon Mitchell, Bobby Astyr

There's a reason why so many porn films from the Golden Age are so highly regarded nowadays, especially by a growing number of scribes and aficionados, and that is because titles like **BARBARA BROADCAST** were made during the heyday of experimental smut, and tower high above the hundreds, perhaps thousands of other titles in the adult movie genre.

Nearly all of **BARBARA BROADCAST**'s entire running time revolves around a fictional upscale New York restaurant that caters to a particular clientele, one which seeks no-holds-barred—as well as no-holes-barred—sex. Adding spice to the courses, the staff energetically interacts with the patrons, providing entertainment for all the guests as well as the viewing audience.

It doesn't take long for the sensual water to boil in this pleasing adult movie opus as we meet the trendy and lusty socialite Barbara Broadcast (Annette Haven) being interviewed (mid-bites of light food and cock), by a reporter (C.J. Laing...who never looked as beautiful elsewhere onscreen as she did in this film). Ms. Broadcast appears to be a jet-setting, Xaviera Hollander-type (author Hollander's sex-filled autobiography, *The Happy Hooker*, was popular around this time, and all the rage). C.J.'s interview gets interrupted by a number of people seeking autographs, and blow jobs...and it's around this point that the camera spends time with some of the restaurant's wait staff as mishandled food or less-than-ideal service is met with a disciplinary action unzip and fuck from maître'd Bobby Astyr.

There's steamy and imaginary fucking in the kitchen; there's a disco nightclub jaunt which finds our star Barbara (Haven) and her now-attached-at-the-hip, pouty-lipped cohort-in-lust C.J. experience Jamie Gillis, who then entertains with a story about him and Constance Money!

High definition erotica from Radley Metzger

Obvious orgasmic pleasures await one of the actresses from **BARBARA BROADCAST**

One of the most outrageous and well-photographed additions to the pornography canon, **BROADCAST** is one of director Metzger's real triumphs when making adult films. The Blu-ray special release from Distribpix is truly astounding and a real collector's item for fans of Golden Age porn. One thing most notable right away is how colorful and clear the whole movie looks, with outrageous natural skin tones literally popping off the screen, no doubt helped by the 2K High Definition transfer job. Besides the Blu-ray disc, there's also a second disc that contains an uncut version in DVD format with a number of extras including a 30-minute interview with Michael Gaunt (a.k.a. Michael Datorre), who recalls his appearance in this movie, as well as other adult titles he's been in and other oddities (he can easily be seen in the opening scenes of Fulci's **GATES OF HELL**!).

And, there's a third disc which contains the substantially reworked (but shorter by seven minutes) softcore version, which excises the graphic footage, and replaces it with narration from an Annette Haven impersonator, an entirely new opening scene, a whole section featuring Robert Bolla/Kerman and a comely young girl at a movie theatre, and more. I guess one had to replace all those well-choreographed but graphic fucking scenes with something.

Still more extras include *A Tribute to the Players*, a nearly twenty-minute look at the key performers in the movie (Besides Haven and Laing, there's also acknowledgements of Sue McBain and Bobby Astyr) narrated by Gaunt. Nearly forty minutes of outtakes, tons of trailers for other Henry Paris/Radley Metzger titles, and more.

Definitely one to have in the collection of every serious purveyor of smut and lovers of Golden Age erotica everywhere…and yeah, the movie's not bad either.

1977, USA. D: HENRY PARIS [RADLEY METZGER]
AVAILABLE FROM DISTRIBPIX [OOP]

WANDA WHIPS WALL STREET

1981, USA. D: Larry Revene
S: *Veronica Hart (a.k.a. Jane Hamilton), Tish Ambrose, Sharon Mitchell, Jamie Gillis, Ron Jeremy*

There are not too many X-rated films from the prime period (or Golden Age, if you will) of adult cinema that one could say that the R-rated version plays just as well as the hardcore one, but this film joins a special circle of movies so well-regarded for their story, acting, and cinematography, that separated from the graphic sex scenes that appear in them, they play just as well, albeit differently. **ROOMMATES** (1981) photographed by Larry Revene, but direction attributed to Chuck Vincent immediately is another that comes to mind.

An excellent film that defines the attempts to bring the genre to new audiences and gain more critical attention and respect, **WANDA WHIPS WALL STREET** tells the tale of Wanda (Veronica Hart), who works for a small firm seeking to enlarge their clientele by destroying the reputation of their much larger competitors via bribery, and in some cases, using the smoking-hot Hart to infiltrate their rival's corporate headquarters to bed and then blackmail the people in charge.

Hart quickly becomes the go-to gal for the New York-based firm Tyler Securities, but secretly rifles through the company's file cabinets looking for dirt or info on their clients. Deciding to seduce and then blackmail the company president (Peter Johns), she's flummoxed when she finds out he's a dick-swinging swinger on the side, who often entertains the rich and famous at his own palatial estate. When Janie (blonde and bushy Tish Ambrose), who worked for Wanda at her old company, turns up, Wanda enlists her aid in her scheme. An energetic orgy where the duo attempt to seduce, fuck, and blackmail as many participants as possible follows…but then ace investigator Lou Perrini (love that name!), played by Jamie Gillis, who with his partner (a thin, charming Ron Jeremy!) turns up to investigate Tyler's sudden loss of monies in the stock market.

Familiar genre faces Samantha Fox and Sharon Mitchell also turn up for a variety of throwaway scenes as two women who also become involved in the complicated plot. Wanda feels ole Jamie might be getting a tad too suspicious of her actions (and motives), so Wanda engineers a weekend getaway to entice him and Ron (who seems to have a fondness for Tish Ambrose's powerful lip suction method!) but things go awry as tables are turned.

The comedic aspects of the film work quite well, actually; not surprisingly, the cast is more than game in this and all the dramatic elements of the story (after all, Hart and Gillis were two of the better actors in the genre). An R-rated version of **WANDA WHIPS WALL STREET** circulated often during the early days of cable television, and with a slight hint of the original X-rated version (softcore titillation and cutaways here), played quite well. Veronica Hart, while not a stunning beauty, nearly always appeared, as one would say, "unconventionally pretty". Poised and pouty with an unusually pert aquiline nose, medium breasts, and an apparent interest in enthusiastically performing the required sexual scenes before the camera, it was Veronica's apparent wizened intelligence that made her a fan (and critical) favorite. She went on to appear in a number of non-adult titles (some horror movies, and even roles in television). The director, Larry Revene, is well known for his cinematography skills, and directed a small amount of movies (although I'm sure he did do many more using a pseudonym), of which **WANDA** is among his best. The 2014 DVD release form Distribpix features an audio commentary, interviews with director Revene and star Hart, was remastered from original negatives, and looks just great.

1981, USA. D: LARRY REVENE
AVAILABLE FROM DISTRIBPIX

DEVIL'S DUE
1973, USA. D: Ernest Danna
S: *Cindy West, Lisa Grant, Darby Lloyd Rains, Gus Thomas, Tina Russell*

Let's take a look now at a weirder kind of horror porn hybrid, the sex-horror movie **DEVIL'S DUE**, a film shot back in a time where the women were very hairy, proud of it, and flaunted their forest-like bushes in front of the cameras for all to see.

When we first see charming, seemingly naïve auburn-haired Cindy (Cindy West), she's rehearsing a speech in the office of what appears to be her professor or the principal. We spy him spiking her drink and before too long the pervy bastard is plowing her furtive forestry before she runs away. Sobbing and in need of

Top: A classic poster. **Middle:** Veronica Hart in a scene from **WANDA WHIPS WALL STREET**. **Above:** Cindy West in **DEVIL'S DUE**

41

Who said the Devil was a man?

a shoulder to cry on, she fucks her mechanic boyfriend Willie, and afterwards tells him she's pregnant (which she believes happened when she was assaulted at the school). Willie's a bozo, so he just laughs it off. When a distraught Cindy tries to find solace in best friend Barbie (Lisa Grant), she's so shocked to find Barbie swallowing her own father's mini-baseball bat-sized schlong that she has a miscarriage, is struck mute…and hops the bus from small-town America to 42nd Street and Times Square.

After quickly meeting Dawn (Andrea True, performing as Catherine Warren) and Nicky (Darby Lloyd Rains, performing as Angel Street) two lesbian roommates who invite Cindy to share their space, she is indoctrinated into the world of black magic and Satan-worshipping.

Kampala (Gus Thomas) claims he's the human-form embodiment of the Devil ("…the spirit of Satan flows through my shaft!"), and wants his girls to go out and trick for him and give him cash, and when they're not doing that, they're chanting along to some nonsense words, before getting down and letting Kampala have his way with them…any which way he wants. There's an energetic orgy near the end featuring a horde of New York-based talent (you can spot Georgina Spelvin, Jamie Gillis, Marc Stevens, and others), but Cindy wisely decides enough is enough and convinces her two gal pals to turn the tables on the wiseass would-be Satanist by getting their own revenge. After Cindy puts poison on her nipples, kills Kampala, and celebrates with a Sapphic three-way, she is anointed the new leader of the cult.

Crazy and threadbare, but never really boring, this is a prime example of cheesy New York-based porn from the earliest days of grindhouse jism-bating. I've not seen the Alpha Blue Archives version of this title, but have read that it's less than an hour long and is minus a lot of footage. The Something Weird Video print, while a bit faded, and what color there is chiefly consists of purples and reds, appears to be longer and more complete. Kudos to them and the late Mike Vraney for preserving prime weird smut for the generations. Available on Something Weird Video's Bucky Beaver's Stags Loops and Peeps Vol. 129.

1973, USA. D: ERNEST DANNA
AVAILABLE FROM SOMETHING WEIRD VIDEO AND ALPHA BLUE ARCHIVES

DISTORTIONS OF REALITY

1972, USA. D: Gary Kahn
S: *Judy Otis, Marc Stevens, Susie Kwan, Karen Cist*

Less fun than **DEVIL'S DUE**, but yet another prime example of the kind of X-rated cinema made on the East Coast in the early 1970s, **DISTORTIONS OF REALITY** has one or two familiar faces (including a young "Mr. 10-inches" Marc Stevens), and yet feels like it's the result of someone cobbling together a series of short, originally silent loops, and then laying a dubbed track over them

to call it a movie in order to get it shown in the X movie theaters that were springing up all over the country.

Seemingly influenced by the then-interest in swinging sex couples, sexual group therapy sessions, and a number of then-popular underground sexual tropes that were just starting to come out of the closet at the dawn of the 'Seventies, **DISTORTIONS** begins as seedier nighttime travelogue of the Times Square area and then segues to Elaine (Judy Otis) being sexually assaulted by a knife-wielding goon. She takes her sad story to her group therapy session but they don't really seem interested. Instead, Alice (Susie Kwan) tells how her performance on a softcore movie set led to her being assaulted by crew member Herb (Pete Rickles). Before everyone gets excited, Ms. Kwan does not in the least appear to be Asian and instead is played by a skanky brunette with a prominent hairy bush. After her tale, it's Herb's turn to tell his version, and in his story…Alice seduced *him*.

Just as boredom sets in, we now have a young Marc Stevens complaining to the group that he thinks his wife (Karen Cist…*really!*) is a lesbian. A cheesy flashback finds Karen discovering the family maid trying out one of those big archaic plastic vibrators, getting turned on herself…and another tryst begins. Fans of hairy brunette girls of the early '70s will have a field day with this one as Stevens pretends to get in on the act by filming the whole thing. Uh, wasn't he complaining a minute ago? Things come to quite a head when Alice (remember her? She's the defacto star of this mess) is hypnotized by the leader of the group (a psychiatrist, I assumed) and is force-fed his manly sausage in an attempt to cure her. In no time, the camera spins around in a dizzying fashion and everybody fucks. The End.

The thing about this porno quickie, terms like "good movie", "exciting", "titillating", and "arousing" are just not warranted here as there's little that applies. Still, it has value as a rare glimpse of early erotica, before better films by talented filmmakers (and in some cases, actors) changed the whole scene. A largely color-faded, damaged print is the way **DISTORTIONS** is presented here on Something Weird Video's Bucky Beaver's Stags Loops and Peeps Vol. 173, but that's half the charm in seeing an obscure movie like this.

1972, USA. D: GARY KAHN
AVAILABLE FROM SOMETHING WEIRD VIDEO

TEENIE TULIP

1970, USA. D: Gerard Damiano
S: *Peggy Simpson, Steve Dickinson, Linda Southern, Georgina Spelvin.*

According to oral histories on the genre and statements made by Georgina Spelvin herself in her own autobiography, she really didn't start appearing in hardcore films until around the time of **DEVIL IN MISS JONES** (1973) for this movie's director Damiano, and yet, she keeps on turning up in X-rated movies made earlier… like this one.

One of the most common plots used in some of the earliest hardcore films is the doctor's office (used to better effect elsewhere), but this one is entertaining in its own archaic way. We pick up our story with MILF-type Karen (Peggy Simpson), who isn't ready to let her fiancé (sporting a very dashing porno mustache) have sex with her prior to their wedding. Her swinger best friend (Linda Southern) suggests that Karen see a doctor for her problems, otherwise she will lose boyfriend Jim to someone who is willing to let him plunge their love canal.

Dr. Luv (played by someone I don't recognize at all, and I've seen a lot of adult films from this period) is a sex therapist (of course) and we quickly learn that Karen was traumatized by an incident in her youth where a friend got excited and forced his dick into her mouth, erupting all over her face. Karen's been scarred ever since.

Dr. Luv has another patient, a male, introduce Karen (and her amazingly dark hairy bush…you can cut through this thing with a lawnmower, folks!) to the joys of sex…but even after she tells her fiancé that she is now an uninhibited walking human wet sponge, she still won't let him have sex with her.

A light bondage scene with an older woman who whips her ass, leading to vibrator abuse and an unsteady lesbian encounter, is followed by a group sex scene and then Dr. Luv proclaims his love to Karen…and surprise-surprise, Dr. Luv isn't who we thought he was after all.

TEENIE TULIP is another gem from the folks at SWV, who thankfully are transferring and archiving early smut from decades ago just so people like us can see how filmmakers during this period balanced comedy and sex.

1970, USA. D: GERARD DAMIANO
AVAILABLE FROM SOMETHING WEIRD VIDEO

THE VIOLATION OF CLAUDIA

1977, USA. D: Billy Bagg (a.k.a. William Lustig)
S: Sharon Mitchell, Jamie Gillis, Don Peterson

THE VIOLATION OF CLAUDIA is directed by big Bill Lustig, known moreover as the director of a number of fondly recalled horror and exploitation movies (**MANIAC** [1980] with Joe Spinell, **VIGILANTE** [1983], **MANIAC COP** [1988] and its sequels), and of course, he's the big guy who runs Blue Underground video company, and as an exploitation movie fan, he's been releasing some of the more obscure DVD and Blu-Ray titles on the market. **VIOLATION** is one of his earliest movies (he directed quite a few using the Billy Bagg alias) and it's quite a good little movie.

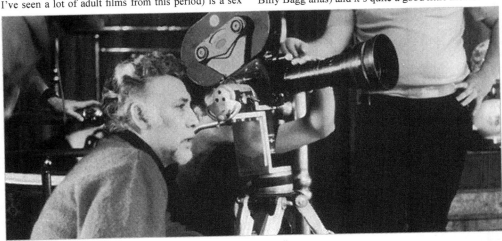

Gerard Damiano directs

We are first introduced to Claudia (Sharon Mitchell), the sexually dissatisfied wife of a prominent politician (Don Peterson), early on as we find her husband, who appears quite wealthy, gives her anything she wants, but has little personal time for her.

Claudia enjoys lunches with her gal pals, who recommend she take up tennis lessons with Kip (Jamie Gillis), a handsome instructor with cock-stuffed shorts who gives her a massage rubdown that leads to quite a scintillating scene in the locker room.

Sensing there's a lot of sexiness in the thin-but-hot body of Claudia, Kip convinces her to be an escort (he's got a number of sexually repressed women working for him, it turns out). One of Claudia's first customers is an older overweight schlub who pours dessert all over Claudia, but she gets into it just the same. To get the sour taste of that experience out of her mouth, she invites a hitchhiker back home and shows him a good time.

More sexual encounters follow, until Claudia decides she's had enough and will go to her husband and tell him all about her new life, in an effort to save their marriage…only to find him in bed with Jamie Gillis!

Barley over an hour long, but extremely well-photographed, with attention paid to the script, setting and performances, this is one of the better early adult films. While I was personally never much of a Sharon Mitchell fan as far as eye candy goes, she played the role of Claudia, whose frustration, innocence and desire are all well-conveyed. Jamie Gillis steals the film by slyly making the role of the suave lover-*cum*-pimp one of his best in the genre.

1977, USA. D: BILLY BAGG [WILLIAM LUSTIG]
AVAILABLE FROM DISTRIBPIX/SWEETHEART
THEATERS

HOT HONEY

1978, USA. D: Billy Bagg (a.k.a. William Lustig)
S: Heather Young (a.k.a. Colleen Anderson), Jamie Gillis, Serena, Lisa Marks, Robyn Bird

HOT HONEY is a darker film that I prefer even more than the previously mentioned title. A seedier look at the "repressed woman" angle than we've been used to in the genre beforehand, it crams a lot of sex action into its all-too-brief 72-minute running time. Honey (Heather Young) is a comely mature woman (somewhere in her early thirties, I would presume, older than the usual X-rated starlets who were in their mid-twenties at the most…save for a few "names" like Georgina Spelvin, Jennifer Welles, and others) who is repressed sexually, claims she is a virgin and just cannot get it together in bed to excite her lover, Johnny (played by the hilariously named Jack Hammer!). He walks out on her after he finds someone who can willfully clean his pipes.

Walking around in a daze and berating herself for own prudish behavior, Honey stops in to visit best friend Sar-

Sharon Mitchell cleanses her body before awaiting another lover in **THE VIOLATION OF CLAUDIA**

ah (Lisa Marks) who alleviates her pent-up frustration by stimulating her moist vagina with a warm bubble bath first, and her tongue second. Honey then visits her sadistic, berating wheelchair-bound brother Jamie Gillis (uh-oh), who has his own personal nurse (Serena). Spying on Jamie and Serena going at it (miraculously, the power of Serena's love juices and mouth seem to have cured Jamie's apparent paralysis!) gets Honey all wet, and something snaps in her, and she joins the fornicating duo. Maybe I missed a transition scene here, or I blinked and then suddenly the small apartment is filled with a number of fornicating women (a young Jeanne Silver among them)…or was Honey just fantasizing?

Returning to Johnny, Honey is eager to please him, and she does. But it's not enough, so after she slathers ac-

Heather Young and lover Jack Hammer enjoy a stroll before Heather's life takes a tenacious turn into lust and depravity in **HOT HONEY**

tual honey on her body and gets aroused, she returns to gal friend Sarah, and gets into bed with her and her husband (Herschel Savage). The End.

Surprisingly, Heather Young is fine in the role of Honey when she's not engaged in the sex scenes. When those

occur, it appears she needs a bit of prompting to unwind. Oddly enough, this reflects the character she's actually playing. Gillis and Serena (who according to Lustig, filmed their role in one day!), who were real-life partners at this time, exhibit some actual heat into their scenes with Young…but such as it is, the movie feels a tad overlong, whereas Lustig's other (and more well-known) adult film **THE VIOLATION OF CLAUDIA** (1977) feels like it could have been longer.

Distribpix are to be applauded for releasing really nice prints of these films (available as their Billy Bagg Double Feature DVD), having restored them in a way that makes the colors (**VIOLATION** was shot in technicolor, which really enhances those flesh tones) pop out in a way that makes the movie seem timeless. There are a few extras, including audio commentary tracks for each, with Lustig moderated by Danish filmmaker Nicholas Winding Refn, who notes it is a personal favorite in his credits.

1978, USA. D: WILLIAM LUSTIG
AVAILABLE FROM
DISTRIBPIX/SWEETHEART THEATERS

WHEN A YOUNG GIRL's GROWING PAINS… BECOME THE PLEASURES OF A WOMAN!

"Surefire!"

"Filled with flesh and fresh faces. An Evelyn Wood crash-speed course in the joys of sex."

NO ONE UNDER 17 ADMITTED

Introducing
Heather Young
Starring
Jamie Gillis · Serena · Simone Sinclair · Jack Hammer
Robin Bird · Bill Berry
Music by Chris D'Antoni · Richard Rau · Written by Travis Webb and
Billy Bagg · Produced and directed by Billy Bagg
Technicolor

GREEK VHS MAYHEM:
Jean Rollin Special
(With a Little Lieberman Love)

by Christos Mouroukis

Back when I was at film school, a fellow student confessed to me that he cannot watch old films, especially those that were shot in black and white. I was shocked, because for one I love oldies, especially black and white goodies, and also because...you know, how can you be a film student and ignore something because it's old? I mean, I understand how my young brother can't watch anything pre-'80s, because he's more into video games, but a film student?

Having said the above, I must also say that I find oppressive the fact that I can't share my love for VHS with many. I often have people at home and we eat pizza, drink beer, and watch the occasional flick, but it always has to be on Blu-ray, or maybe DVD—never on VHS. People tell me they can't stand the shit quality of tapes. People became so used to HD, DVDs, Blu-ray and what not that they are ready to ignore films just because they are in a now-alien format.

Don't get me wrong, I too suffer each time I have to clean up my old VCR in order to watch a tape, but recently I found out that there are online communities of people who won't watch something if it's not on Blu-ray. To me, regardless of the format, a good film is a good film; an entertaining film is an entertaining film...and so on. The copy doesn't have to be perfect. But, okay, it has to be uncut.

This installment of the Greek VHS Mayhem column is dedicated to Jean Rollin, my favorite French director.

My first Jean Rollin experience was at a very young age (something like 12 years old), when in the first video store I was frequenting I noticed the terrifying cover of **THE NIGHT OF THE HUNTED** (1980), in which a scissor penetrates the eyes of an unlucky girl. I was too horrified to dare to rent it, even though the clerks would have let me, since they never seemed to care about what went into my VCR.

Fast-forward a few years and when the video stores started shutting down I managed to add **THE NIGHT OF THE HUNTED** and six more Greek ex-rental original Jean Rollin VHS tapes to my collection. Most of them were released by the same distributor (Sunset Video).

Jean Rollin to me is the best thing to ever come out of France when it comes to arts, and his poetic masterpieces hold a big portion of my collection, especially on DVD. Coming from France, most of his films are better viewed with a glass of good French wine.

To be fair, it should be mentioned that Jean Rollin directed his fair share of adult films in order to pay his bills, and although I've seen some of it, I never managed to track down Jean Rollin porn on Greek VHS. I believe that some of it was out there, but I cannot confirm that.

The late Jean Rollin, *ca.* 1998

47

Anyway, on with the article: get your wine, smoke cigarettes, and enjoy celluloid poetry at its finest, along with vampirism and other awesomeness of the dark.

(And since space permits us I threw in a couple of Jeff Lieberman films reviews, too.)

JEAN ROLLIN CHAPTER

LES DÉMONIAQUES
(a.k.a. THE DEMONIACS, a.k.a. CURSE OF THE LIVING DEAD)

Just before the beginning credits we are introduced to a bunch of northern seas pirates (I hate to say it, but they look unintentionally hilarious). Straight after the credits we are introduced to the title's girls. Those two beautiful girls appear dressed in white and ask for help from the bandits. The dirty men shoot them and rape them and leave them for dead. Soon the girls will return as ghosts to hunt them and get their bloody revenge. They will also reveal the cursed village's horrible secret. There is also something going on with a weird clown, but don't ask. As with most writer/director Jean Rollin flicks, this one is best remembered for the excellent use of locations.

1974, FRANCE/BELGIUM. D: JEAN ROLLIN
AVAILABLE FROM KINO LORBER/REDEMPTION

LÈVRES DE SANG
(a.k.a. LIPS OF BLOOD, a.k.a. SUCK ME, VAMPIRE)

In a party for the high society in a Paris apartment, the male lead Frédéric (Jean-Loup Philippe from KILLING CAR [1993]) sees a picture of a castle on the wall which brings him memories of his first love. We see those via flashbacks. He gets creative and tracks down the photographer who tells him where the mysterious castle is, but first she has her way with him.

Frédéric finally goes to the castle (which comes complete with a spooky cemetery in which the filmmakers reportedly filmed without a permission), and he finds the lady he fell in love with when he was a child. The thing is…he also finds bats in coffins, and vampires. Yes, said vampires are female and sexy. And yes, said vampires wear see-through robes. The vampires get to do some killing, but things get really complicated from this point onwards, and it'll be better for you to watch it and make your own conclusions. Essentially this is a love story with vampirism thrown in, and the best thing

Left: Greek VHS video covers for Rollin's **THE DEMONIACS** (*top*) and **LIPS OF BLOOD** (*bottom*)

about it is the creepy and monotonous music (by Didier William Lepauw).

1975, FRANCE. D: JEAN ROLLIN
AVAILABLE FROM KINO LORBER/REDEMPTION

LA NUIT DES TRAQUÉES
(a.k.a. **THE NIGHT OF THE HUNTED**)

Robert (Vincent Gardère) finds a young woman (Brigitte Lahaie) wandering in the night, in the middle of nowhere. He wants to take her to Paris, which is only two hours' drive away. She doesn't want to go, but she doesn't know where she lives either, so she takes the ride.

The couple arrives in Paris and make love in Robert's apartment. Meanwhile, mysterious people are spying on them (they are interested in capturing the girl). When Robert leaves his flat, the bad guys enter and kidnap the young lady. They imprison her in a modern tower, where she will stay with some other inmates. Why they all are kept there? Why do they have memory loss? Will they be able to escape?

This is essentially another love story (if you don't believe me, check out the finale) with conspiracy theories thrown in for good measure. It is the first Jean Rollin film I fell in love with, and I still admire it as a great piece of high art. The copy reviewed here is in French language with Greek subtitles. Said subtitles are of yellow colour, which is a rarity with Greek VHS tapes.

1980, FRANCE. D: JEAN ROLLIN
AVAILABLE FROM KINO LORBER/REDEMPTION

LE LAC DES MORTS VIVANTS
(a.k.a. **ZOMBIE LAKE**)

Real phone call transcription:[1]
> Eurocine (production company): "Mr. Rollin, would you please come down and shoot a shit zombie script for us, because Jess Franco who was attached disappeared?"
> Jean Rollin: "Only if I can use my J.A. Laser pseudonym."

A girl swims at the title's lake (I don't speak French, but I can tell that it translates as *"Lake of the Living Dead"*)…and soon she gets attacked by zombies in Nazi uniforms! The townsfolk worry about the girl's disappearance and so does their mayor (Howard Vernon), who is concerned, but he seems like he knows stuff. Meanwhile, the zombies carry on with the attacking business.

---

1 Well, it's not real, but the essential story is true.

Right: Gruesome images adorn the Greek VHS covers for **NIGHT OF THE HUNTED** (*top*) and **ZOMBIE LAKE** (*bottom*)

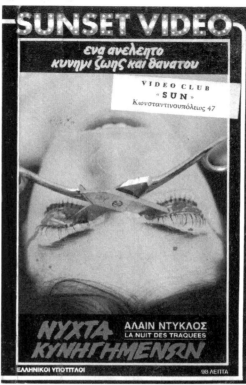

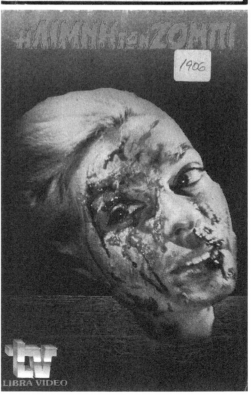

A blonde (but unattractive) female reporter comes to the village and wants to write a story about what she calls "Lake of Ghosts". The mayor corrects her and calls the place "The Lake of the Damned". Whatever you want to call the place (the print under review bears the title **ZOMBIES' LAKE**), it is soon visited by a team of female basketball players (who are not very convincing, as they don't seem to be comfortable with the ball). Said players are soon slaughtered by the Nazi zombies.

Now, the mayor will let us know of the lake's secrets via a lengthy flashback that reveals WWII stuff, in which the locals threw Nazi soldiers' bodies in the lake (well, there's not many of them, so the whole thing is very **PLAN 9 FROM OUTER SPACE** [1959]). There is also a love story between a villager and a soldier. Once the flashback is over we will see this particular zombie finding and protecting his living young daughter. Well, modern fathers are indeed zombies, so the scene doesn't seem that bizarre or ridiculous. No, it does, but…oh, well.

Two inspectors are assigned to the case (one of them is played by director Jean Rollin) and once they approach the lake they are murdered by the Nazi zombies. Well, that's all the locals can take, and they decide to take the law into their own hands. I'm not going to reveal the ending, because if you haven't seen the flick I would spoil the great fun the protagonists' plan provides. The only thing I want to add about it is this priceless line: "Don't forget me. I won't forget".

Well, hipsters found out that dead Nazis can come back from their graves through modern films such as **DØD SNØ** (a.k.a. **DEAD SNOW**, 2009) and **IRON SKY** (2012), but those in the know were always aware of this little gem. It is generally considered one of the worst zombie films ever made, but I find it very entertaining, and that's all a movie needs, really.

1981, FRANCE/SPAIN. D: JEAN ROLLIN
AVAILABLE FROM KINO LORBER/REDEMPTION

LES PAUMÉES DU PETIT MATIN
(a.k.a. **THE ESCAPEES**, a.k.a. **THE RUNAWAYS**)

Two young girls escape from psychiatric clinic and soon join a travelling burlesque act. The road to ruin is full of good intentions, such as alcohol and sexual adventures. One of the girls is afraid of people, while the other one simply wants to have fun. They are very different and the character development in this film is excellent. Their journey will bring them very close together, and if you can sit through this lengthy drama (the copy reviewed here is 100 minutes long), you will be rewarded with a poetic and spectacular ending. Brigitte Lahaie appears

Left: Covers for **THE ESCAPEES** (*top*) and **THE LIVING DEAD GIRL** (*bottom*)

late in the film, in a small but important role, and director Rollin makes a blink-and-you'll-miss-it cameo. Once I finished watching the film for the purpose of this review, the VCR chewed up the tape. How Rock 'n' Roll is that?

1981, FRANCE. D: JEAN ROLLIN
AVAILABLE FROM KINO LORBER/REDEMPTION

LA MORTE VIVANTE
(a.k.a. **THE LIVING DEAD GIRL**)

In dark catacombs, two guys dispose of chemical waste. They also find the time to do some grave-robbing (in order to steal jewellery). The dead bodies seem fresh and the coffins look new. Unfortunately for them, there's an earthquake, which spills the toxic waste all over the place, which on the one hand kills one of the guys, and on the other hand resurrects a beautiful blonde girl (Françoise Blanchard from **LES TROTTOIRS DE BANGKOK** [a.k.a. **SIDEWALKS OF BANGKOK**, 1984]—see below), who as a zombie goes on a killing spree.

A photographer happens to catch the female zombie on film, and she does some research about her in the nearby village. One of the guys she asks information from at the flea market is Jean Rollin, in one of his usual cameos.

Well, this is the closest director Jean Rollin ever came to making a conventional horror film (at least for the era), and this is because it is certainly his goriest work (especially during the first half and the last minutes), accompanied with the necessary gratuitous nudity. And this is probably why it is his most widely seen film.

More than a decade ago, I used to sing for a black metal band, and we named one song after this film's title. I can't speak French, so the whole thing was done with an Italian accent. Since then I stopped singing and I only play the drums...and I do that in a punk rock band. Oh, and guess what, once I finished watching the film for the purpose of this review, the VCR chewed up this tape, too. I know, I know...the Rock 'n' Roll of the analogue technology...

1982, FRANCE. D: JEAN ROLLIN
AVAILABLE FROM KINO LORBER/REDEMPTION

LES TROTTOIRS DE BANGKOK
(a.k.a. **SIDEWALKS OF BANGKOK**)

In the first minutes of this movie we get to meet Rick, who is a spy but his cover is a film camera with which he claims he's making a folklore flick. Rick gets killed and his film ends up in Paris with the good guys. Two girls enter their headquarters and steal the film. From then on the action moves to Bangkok. Well, "action" is not really the proper word, as all the so-called action sequences are lousy. The gratuitous nudity is what makes this movie watchable. It is the director's least personal film among

SIDEWALKS OF BANGKOK, Greek VHS-style!

the ones reviewed here, and it is the closest he ever got to a mainstream spy/action flick. Oh, and a film theatre in the movie showcases a big poster of **ORCA** (1977).

1984, FRANCE. D: JEAN ROLLIN
AVAILABLE FROM IMAGE/REDEMPTION

JEFF LIEBERMAN CHAPTER

SQUIRM

On the 29th of September, 1975, a reckless storm hit Georgia. Along with the numerous disasters it also brought up deadly worms. Mick (Don Scardino from **CRUISING** [1980], who got the part because Martin Sheen did not) arrives at the place to have a good time. He soon finds trouble because some of the locals despise the fact that he's from the big city (at a cafe, he orders a drink, in which he finds a worm, and the bartender and sheriff put the blame on him). Luckily, Geri (Patricia Pearcy, who got the role that Kim Basinger first auditioned for) will be there for him. Anyway, the two friends soon come across some human bones. They go and bring the sheriff to check them out, but once the three of them are back at the scene, the body is missing.

The rest of the film (which was shot in less than 25 days) is about worms (who sound like pigs and this is because

in the sound design actual pig sounds were used) attacking human beings, and the lead couple uncovering the mystery. The most effective scenes are the ones that take place in familiar settings such as bathrooms (because this could happen to any member of the audience)—those are indeed some scary scenes, or at least disgusting (in a squirmy way). Some of the practical effects are excellent, and the suspense builds up nicely thanks to the fantastic original score by Robert Prince.

Reportedly, Jeff Lieberman encourages viewers to watch this flick in black and white. I've seen it a couple of times but always in colour. The cinematography by Joseph Mangine (who also shot my personal favourite, **ALONE IN THE DARK** [1982]) is such that I cannot personally recommend any changes.

The best thing about this release is the box cover. I mean, take a look; you can't forget such brilliant artwork. There are some things you cannot un-see. But if I had time in my life for only one '70s worm-themed US movie, I would prefer to watch **THE WORM EATERS** (1977) by Ted Mikels instead, because it is really far more entertaining. But I don't have a life, so I've seen both a couple of times. I hope there will come a day in which I will be able to review films without actually having to watch them…wait a minute—some reviewers do that already, right?

1976, USA. D: JEFF LIEBERMAN
AVAILABLE FROM MGM AND SHOUT! FACTORY

JUST BEFORE DAWN

This flick (whose original working title was THE LAST RITUAL) starts with an explosion (of a car) and a murder in a cabin in the woods. There is a survivor from this instance—keep notes. A bunch of young people (well, five of them, actually) arrive in a van, and no matter how much old Roy (George Kennedy) warns them, they go on to camp in the mountain woods.

On their way there they hit a deer…but most importantly, the killer jumps on top of their van. The survivor of the first attack warns them about the "demons" in the area, but they still want to camp there. Once they camp they hear some creepy singing, find where it comes from, see a creepy antisocial girl running in the woods, and still they remain in the area.

Anyway, since they're stubbornly staying in the woods they try to make the most of it, so they swim in the nearby lake, but the hands of the killer grab the booty of the female lead and she panics. They shouldn't worry too much about the antagonist's minor perversions, though,

Left: Thankfully, the Greek VHS for **SQUIRM** (*top*) retained the majority of poster-master Drew Struzan's original artwork, but the same cannot be said for the boring cheapjack cover for **JUST BEFORE DAWN** (*bottom*)

as soon he'll start slashing them off with a big-ass machete. And okay, kids may like **MACHETE** (2010), and Danny Trejo is a nice guy, but the villain here is the real mean deal when it comes to machete-welding lunatics.

But I know what you're thinking: **FRIDAY THE 13TH** (1980). And you are right. Cunningham's slasher epic is even mentioned in the synopsis on the back of the box cover. But as long as this flick is strictly conventional (during the first half), it is really good, while when it gets a bit complicated (during the second half), it gets boring. It also gets too dark to see, especially if you are watching a VHS tape like I did. It is a film that works with what you don't see instead of what you see, and it is scary. The copy I reviewed is the World Video Productions release which runs 89 minutes, whose box cover is not very exciting. My collection also holds the Video City release, which is shorter (running at 86 minutes) but its box artwork is creepy.

1981, USA. D: JEFF LIEBERMAN
AVAILABLE FROM MEDIA BLASTERS AND CODE RED

That's it for now folks! Until next time, happy digging! I know it's lonely, but it's fun...

Jeff Lieberman (photo by Wilhelm Tell)

STEVE'S VIDEO STORE
POST-HALLOWEENIE EDITION 3:
DISNEY HORRORS

by Steven "The Ghoul" Ronquillo

Okay, it's Halloween again, and as usual, I am sitting here with a bowl of candy and a shotgun with rock salt in it. Every year I make a special aisle for Halloween, and this year it's Disney. Yes, I know they are the evil media giant who owns your whole Gen-X childhood, but suck it up, buttercup—we all grew up with these creepy delights, so enjoy my picks and let me take you back...so grab some candy and grab a few titles!

> Let me tell you about my mother...

First up is a couple of what Disney called Silly Symphonies; they were musical-oriented shorts that told a story through animation and music. The first one they ever did was 1929's *The Skeleton Dance*, and it was just skeletons doing creepy dancy things while a xylophone track played on. It worked so well it has been used in many things throughout the years, and it was the very first use of a xylophone in a motion picture, animated or not.

Next is *Hell's Bells* (1929)—no not the AC/DC song, but a creepy Halloween-themed cartoon with the Devil, Cerberus and the Grim Reaper in a spooky little cartoon with various demons from hell! Disney did plenty of shorts like that, even going as far as *Pluto's Judgement Day* (1935), a cartoon envisioning Pluto being sent to a hell with demonic cats galore, and it's amazing. But if you want to talk about scaring galore I will have to tell a story Donnie Dunnigan, voice of the titular fawn in

BAMBI (1942) told me. Paraphrasing Dunnigan: "When I got into the Army, this tough sergeant pulled me aside and asked, 'Did you do the voice of Bambi, son?' 'Sir yes sir!' 'You made me cry, you sonovabitch!'" Yes, the killing of Bambi's mom was a sincerely shocking and horrifying scene that kicked all our asses when we saw it, and Walt himself allegedly called it one of the biggest mistakes he ever made.[1]

Now on to one of my all time faves: "Night on Bald Mountain" from **FANTASIA** (1941). This is so evil and awesome, it has the Devil, demons and witches lording over all while nekkid women (with no clothes

---

1 Some theorize that this famously traumatic cartoon death was motivated by the tragic death of Disney's own mother, Flora Call Disney, who died in 1938 from asphyxiation due to a faulty furnace in a house Walt himself had recently purchased for his parents; this naturally haunted him for the rest of his life. Indeed, dead parents/orphans are an oft-recurring story element/theme in Disney films, from **SNOW WHITE AND THE SEVEN DWARVES** in 1937 on up through 2013's **FROZEN**. *—ed.*

The 1929 Silly Symphony short *Hell's Bells* milks your nightmares for all they're worth!

on!) dance (nude!) in the Devil's hand. And yes, folks, we have nipples in a Disney movie! *YEAAHHHH!* They went so over the top with the imagery that the look of the Devil has been famously used in many places, and Mussorgky's "Night on Bald Mountain" just sounds evil as a musical piece.

Now for the horror classic that is Disney's *The Legend of Sleepy Hollow* (1949). Good god, is this one scary as hell! The last 20 minutes, once Ichabod Crane leaves the party, should be used in film classes to show how to do a perfect subtle gothic horror scene, because the headless horseman himself doesn't show up for the first 10 minutes of it and is only in it at the last little bit, but damn, from his first moment 'til he throws the pumpkin, he's a terror icon!

Next is **CHILD OF GLASS** (1978), a TV movie I saw on *The Wonderful World of Disney* as a kid. This legitimately creepy movie is about a girl's ghost and the boy who gets caught up in her curse that was put on her by her father to make sure her ghost watches over his treasure. The boy

The iconic 1929 Silly Symphony, *The Skeleton Dance*, delivers everything its title promises, and more

has three days to help her find out the secret of "the child of glass" or he will become a ghost, too. This movie uses its N'awlins setting perfectly and was much creepier than expected from a Disney movie from that era, and is a cult fave for kids of my generation who saw it on TV.

Now we are at the late '70s, where Disney tried to make movies for older viewers. An honorable mention goes to **THE BLACK HOLE** (1979) for how creepy the first bit is, where they are exploring the seemingly abandoned ship... that segment oozes atmosphere and creepiness.

And now for the '80s, with two very good creepers that Disney put out that decade. The first is **THE WATCHER IN THE WOODS** (1980), about two sisters who move into their aunt's house for the summer, and get caught up in a mystery about a girl who got lost in the woods many years ago. This is a very, very non-Disney movie with its creepiness.[2] This film also has an odd production legacy, resulting in there being three endings to it, and two entirely different credit sequences. From a glowing entity called "The Watcher" to the original ending featuring an alien with a broken space ship (seriously!), this is a wild mix with and strange history, where the final result is an awesome little movie

By the pricking of my thumb, it's time to talk about **SOMETHING WICKED THIS WAY COMES** (1983)! This is an adaption of Ray Bradbury's novel about a ghostly carnival led by Mr. Dark (a perfectly cast Johnathan Pryce) which comes into town one dark

---

2   In the film's original theatrical release, the Disney name was greatly downplayed on prints, posters and ads, due to the film's dark nature and the PG-rating. They have since claimed greater ownership of it, and now proudly emblazon its graphic materials with the Disney logo. *–ed.*

night bringing temptation and evil with it. This is not a perfect film; it does have its problems, but is that from the extensive reshoots or the other meddling Disney did? Either way, any movie where Pam Grier is cast as the most beautiful woman in the world is perfect.

Well that's it for this post-Halloween edition of Steve's Video Store! Happy Halloween! Be sure to check one or more of these fearsome flicks out, and always remember…

Always keep looking. There are always new titles to find.

Be nice to the new fans. Because you were once a wet-behind-the-ears fan yourself.

Embrace the past. But don't drown it in nostalgia.

…And always remember: it's our love that keeps these movies alive more than anything else, so keep scanning the shelves!

————

The Skeleton Dance
1929, USA. D: WALT DISNEY
RELEASED BY BUENA VISTA [OOP]

Hell's Bells
1929, USA. D: UB IWERKS
RELEASED BY BUENA VISTA [OOP]

Pluto's Judgement Day
1935, USA. D: DAVID HAND
RELEASED BY BUENA VISTA [OOP]

BAMBI
1942, USA. D: JAMES ALGAR, SAMUEL ARMSTRONG, DAVID HAND, GRAHAM HEID, BILL ROBERTS, PAUL SATTERFIELD, NORMAN WRIGHT
AVAILABLE FROM WALT DISNEY

FANTASIA
1940, USA. D: NORMAN FERGUSON, JAMES ALGAR, SAMUEL ARMSTRONG, FORD BEEBE JR., JIM HANDLEY, T. HEE, WILFRED JACKSON ("NIGHT ON BALD MOUNTAIN" SEQUENCE), HAMILTON LUSKE, BILL ROBERTS, PAUL SATTERFIELD, BEN SHARPSTEEN
AVAILABLE FROM WALT DISNEY

The Legend of Sleepy Hollow
1949, USA. D: CLYDE GERONIMI, JACK KINNEY
AVAILABLE FROM WALT DISNEY

CHILD OF GLASS
1978, USA. D: JOHN ERMAN
AVAILABLE FROM WALT DISNEY

THE BLACK HOLE
1979, USA. D: GARY NELSON
AVAILABLE FROM WALT DISNEY

THE WATCHER IN THE WOODS
1980, USA. D: JOHN HOUGH, VINCENT McEVEETY
AVAILABLE FROM WALT DISNEY

SOMETHING WICKED THIS WAY COMES
1983, USA. D: JACK CLAYTON
AVAILABLE FROM WALT DISNEY

Lightening rod salesman Tom Fury (Royal Dano) meets his ironic doom at the hands of Mr. Dark (Jonathan Pryce) in **SOMETHING WICKED THIS WAY COMES**

PACHAMAMA FILMS

"Pull-no-punches art undared by ordinary filmmakers... they crawl under my movie radar and jumped me from the inside."

-C. Dean Andersson (author of Torture Tomb

VERMEERWORKS.COM

DEADLY EYES

(a.k.a. **THE RATS**)

Reviewed by Andy Ross

An intelligent and adaptable creature whose physical appearance continues to send shivers down the human spine, the rat has been an integral part of the horror genre almost since the genre's inception. Featured in literature through works of Bram Stoker, H.P. Lovecraft and Stephen King, and on film through the likes of **WILLARD** (1971), **THE FOOD OF THE GODS** (1976), and **GRAVEYARD SHIFT** (1990), the rat was to secure its membership in the horror pantheon via James Herbert's 1974 novel *The Rats*. The first of a trilogy—*The Rats*, *The Lair*, and *Domain*—Herbert's original novel was to revisit the author's East End London roots and his enduring memories of the vermin that dwelt there. Panned by contemporaneous critics due to the author's unpolished and down-to-earth prose, *The Rats* nevertheless was to prove a massive commercial success. Adapted from the source by Charles H. Eglee, the filmic adaptation's shooting script was to affect some rather sweeping changes to the original manuscript. Re-homing the rat population from London to Toronto and weaving in a rather damning commentary on the prevalence of genetically-modified food, as a film that was to employ both POV and costumed dogs to realize its rodent antagonists, **DEADLY EYES** (1982) was a particularly memorable entry to the "man versus nature" subgenre.

Concerned when a shipment of genetically modified corn reveals evidence of rodent infestation, dedicated health inspector Kelly Leonard (Sara Botsford of **TREMORS 4: THE LEGEND BEGINS** [2004]) insists that the consignment be written-off. In the interim, the local rat population has been gorging itself on the contaminated produce and, as a result, has grown oversized and unbelievably aggressive. With the slaughter of George Foskins' (Scatman Crothers of **THE SHINING** [1980]) cat providing little more than a canapé, the rats begin to utilize the city's sewer system as a means of patrolling the local area. When an attack on a toddler and his teenaged sister reveals the organized nature of the rat pack, the menace is brought to Kelly's attention after one of Paul Harris' (Sam Groom from **DEADLY GAMES** [1982]) students is bitten by an unseen assailant. With medics at a loss to identify the attacker—an animal with the bite-force of a dog but with the dental structure of a rodent—Kelly deploys Foskins, her field technician, to gather evidence of a possible underground lair. Discovering far more than he bargained for, the old man's escape is cut short when the rats converge on him from all sides. Trapped and bleeding out, there is little George can do but await his grisly demise. With evidence of an infestation mounting, Paul contacts his old friend Dr. Spencer (Cec Linder, from **LOLITA** [1962]), whose vast knowledge of the creature leads him to conclude that the steroids used in the corn shipment have effectively created a new breed of "super-rat". When an attempt to fumigate the sewers leads to a mass migration of the killer rodents, the city's unwitting populace provides a catharsis for their revenge.

Having fallen in love with Kelly, Paul allows his young son Tim (Lee-Max Walton) to accompany her to the unveiling of a new station in the city's subway system. An exciting event for the train-mad youngster and a potential vote-winner for the incumbent (stereotypically crooked) mayor, the inaugural journey is swiftly cut short when the rats chew through the power supply, immobilizing a train. Forced to leave their carriages, and frighteningly vulnerable, the passengers begin to edge their way through the clinging darkness. Seizing the moment, the rats launch a concerted attack on the hopelessly-inconvenienced passengers…

Best described as a contemporary take on "Atomic Age" creature features, **DEADLY EYES** serves to question Man's interference in the natural order of things. That the mutant rats wreaking havoc on the city have evolved as a direct result of genetic experimentation makes them far less the Devil than it does the Devil's advocates. Combining the rat's natural intelligence and survival instinct with increased size and appetite, the most convenient (and prevalent) food source becomes man himself, and it's an aspect of the film that produces its most memorable and bloody set-pieces. As the film's most effective set-piece—the rats attacking patrons in a movie theatre, much like the scene in **GREMLINS** (1984) when the mischievous title critters are enjoying an exclusive screening of **SNOW WHITE AND THE SEVEN DWARFS** (1937)—one can imagine audiences peering into the gloom for any fleeting signs of movement. Using puppets for the close-up work and short-legged dachshunds for the distance shots, the rats in **DEADLY EYES** (when not heard barking excitedly!) are particularly effective. When cheerleader Trudy's (Lisa Langlois from **HAPPY BIRTHDAY TO ME** [1981]) attempts at seducing Paul fail miserably, the pretty blonde reunites with her on-and-off boyfriend to take in a Bruce Lee retrospective. Finally commanding his attention over the onscreen action of **GAME OF DEATH** (死亡游戏 / *Si wang you xi*, 1978) as Trudy's beau places his popcorn on the floor (freeing his hands for the task ahead) the first of the rats makes its move. A marvelous scene of teenage carnage accompanied by John Barry's memorable score, in true falling dominoes fashion, those successfully fleeing the rodents are swiftly trodden underfoot.

As a film that evokes the scary fun theme of Halloween, **DEADLY EYES** would be a worthy addition to any network's seasonal scheduling. With liberal helpings of gore, panic-stricken teens and an engaging—albeit predictable—narrative, **DEADLY EYES**' avoidance of explicit sexual imagery makes it the perfect popcorn horror flick. Co-produced by Golden Harvest (the Hong Kong-based studio that kick-started Bruce Lee's career), whilst **DEADLY EYES** was to forge convenient relationships between its cast of characters (e.g., an elderly man slain in the park has been romancing Kelly's sweet, silver-haired neighbor; the bitten boy is none other than Paul's star basketball player) and frequently telegraph its intentions (e.g., Paul's students deciding to pay an untimely visit to the movies; Kelly's invitation to attend the subway opening), fans of easily-digestible '80s shock cinema will readily devour it.

1982, CANADA/HONG KONG.
D: ROBERT CLOUSE
AVAILABLE FROM SHOUT! FACTORY

YELLOWBRICKROAD

Reviewed by Tony Strauss

This creepy little festival sleeper from first-time writer/director team Jesse Holland and Andy Mitton is a film that really has its work cut out for it. The premise and setup will inevitably conjure up knee-jerk, dismissive comparisons to **THE BLAIR WITCH PROJECT** (1999) before one's even seen the film itself. The slow-burn, character-driven storyline will put off much of today's ADHD Generation of viewers accustomed to blaring metal soundtracks and rapid-fire jump shocks. The film provides no easy answers for the casual viewer seeking simple escapist thrills. This is a film destined to divide audiences in a hurry. And it happens to be one of the best *genuine horror* films of its time.

The opening title cards inform us that "One morning in 1940, the entire population of Friar, New Hampshire, walked north up an unmarked trail into the wilderness. Some were later found frozen to death. Others were mysteriously slaughtered. Most, however, were never found." Period photos from the area depict the citizenry as seemingly normal people who inexplicably vanished en masse in an exodus from their quaint New England hometown. We see some of the bodies that were found, and we hear a horrified and jumbled audio interview from the only survivor.

Over the subsequent seven decades, the unsolved case quietly metamorphosed into a legend mostly unknown outside of Friar, and the eventually repopulated town's

DEADLY EYES German poster

THIS ROAD HAS NO FAIRY TALE ENDING

YELLOWBRICKROAD

YELLOWBRICKROAD US poster

residents are hesitant to discuss it with each other, much less with any outsiders.

After years of research and digging, photographer Teddy Barnes (Michael Laurino) believes he has enough information surrounding this mysterious event to undertake the writing of a book with his wife and co-author, Melissa (Anessa Ramsey). They assemble a team of experts to lead on an excursion first into Friar, and then into the woods that supposedly claimed the town's original residents.

Accompanied by sibling map-makers Erin and Daryl (real-life siblings Cassidy and Clark Freeman), their behavioral psychologist friend Walter (Alex Draper), Forestry Service guide Cy (Sam Elmore), and intern Jill (Tara Giordano), they arrive in Friar to find their prospects dampened almost immediately. Nobody in town wants them there, and the trailhead coordinates they've been given are for the town's movie theatre. It is only after giving in to the "take me with you" demands of the theatre's snack bar worker Liv (Laura Heisler) that they are even able to verify that the legendary trail actually exists.

Once underway, things seem innocuous enough, and even when odd things do start happening (such as the fact that Jill's GPS begins to think they're globe-trotting), they don't seem terribly foreboding. But the farther the trail takes them, the more unsettling their environment becomes; the more they need to band together as a group, the more their emotions begin to push at one another. By the time they start to hear faint, pleasant music echoing through the trees, they may no longer even be operating under their own wills, and the worst aspects of their own psyches are rapidly boiling to the surface. The goal of finding the trail's end becomes overshadowed by their desperate fight to maintain their sanity and survive the inimical influences of the forces surrounding them.

A warning to casual viewers: This film is *not* a simple entertainment which will deliver a ribbon-tied story with a tidy ending. It is a horror tale in the *true* Lovecraftian form—that is to say, it isn't a Cthulhu mythos entry or homage, but rather a depiction of the unknowable hostilities that await any foolhardy mortals who dare to hubristically tread where we don't belong. It follows the structure of a majority of Lovecraft's work, in which horror is built by first becoming familiar with the characters (something this film does superbly), and then witnessing subtle intrusions upon the characters' personalities and perceptions, finally resulting in the realization that what they are attempting to accomplish or discover has blinded them to their own ignorance of the true incomprehensible malevolence of the universe, and their own insignificance within it. Pretty heady stuff for what initially seems like just another lost-in-the-woods movie! Ultimately, this film has less in common with **THE BLAIR WITCH PROJECT** than it does with more philosophically ambitious, cosmicism-based genre fare such as Larry Fessenden's **THE LAST WINTER** (2006) and Vincenzo Natali's **CUBE** (1997), and would make a great double-feature viewing paired with Renny Harlin's underrated found-footage spooker **DEVIL'S PASS** (a.k.a. **THE DYATLOV PASS INCIDENT**, 2013).[1]

Fans of more traditional, closed-end horror may feel duped or conned by **YELLOWBRICKROAD** (2010), because it is a deliberate bait-and-switch act: it presents itself as a mystery that the characters (and, by extension, the viewers) intend to solve, then evolves into a tale of mankind's impotence in the face of true, unknowable Mystery. In other words, you may find yourself entertained by and engaged in the search, only to realize, perhaps too late, that you, yourself—just like the film's characters—have been drawn into something much broader and esoteric.

I don't want to give the impression that this is an impenetrable, artsy mindfuck that's just trying to leave you scratching your head. In fact, the actual explanation of the film's events are delivered to the viewer quite efficiently, albeit less in an expository fashion than in a "seeing the big picture", subconscious manner. Indeed, if you listen to the filmmakers' straightforward explanation of the story (found in their engaging and insightful DVD commentary), you'll most likely realize that you'd already figured it out yourself without even realizing it.

Given the premise and situations, many filmmakers in this day and age would have chosen to shoot the film as a found-footage/pseudo-documentary piece, but Holland and Mitton quite wisely chose to shoot in a traditional narrative style, which helps avoid the FF subgenre's annoying and distracting pitfalls of expository "at the camera" narration and fabricating excuses for keeping the

---

1   See review on p.88

characters' cameras on the action, not to mention giving the story a greater resonance as it closes in on its ultimate revelations. Instead, the film is expertly shot, directed and acted—vital to a film that relies this heavily on character and mood—from a solid, intelligent script, and the sound design is truly inspired. Genuine dread is conjured from interactions as mundane as Erin's intense dislike of her brother's hat, or Walter's casual doubting of Liv's honesty. There is not a great deal of violence in the film, but when violence does erupt, it is depicted with an almost dispassionate, matter-of-fact attitude, rendering it far more disturbing and shocking than if it had been lingered on as spectacle. Most impressively, the film never lets you off the hook by allowing you the distancing comfort of omniscience. You never know any more than the characters, and you are bound to experience the same horror they do. This is one of the rare horror films that actually *ends* in horror rather than denouement, which I found to be absolutely (and chillingly) refreshing.

If my assessments and warnings haven't scared you away by this point, and you're the type that enjoys a little challenge in their horrors, then this is probably a film you should seek out immediately. This kind of horror doesn't come along too often, and deserves to be discovered by discerning genre fans. You know who you are. Enjoy your picture show.

2010, USA. D: JESSE HOLLAND, ANDY MITTON
AVAILABLE FROM THE COLLECTIVE

LONG WEEKEND

Reviewed by Jeff Goodhartz

"Ozploitation", a term first coined in Mark Hartley's immensely entertaining documentary, **NOT QUITE HOLLYWOOD: THE WILD, UNTOLD STORY OF OZPLOITATION!** (2008), has quickly become synony-

mous with all manner of Aussie exploitation cinema that exploded in the '70s and '80s. Sex, violence, action, horror: all were presented in the most over-the-top, go-for-broke way imaginable. Some of these exercises in cheap thrills were quite good, while others…not so much. But most all bore the mark of highly enthusiastic filmmakers who seemed blissfully unaware of the word "subtle". It is therefore a surprise when one comes upon a film like **LONG WEEKEND** (1978), which defies genre expectations and presents its audience with something quietly sinister and unnerving as it marks its entrance into the then-popular "nature gone wild" subgenre…or does it?

Peter (John Hargreaves) and Marcia (Briony Behets) are an unhappy and constantly bickering married couple who attempt to salvage their marriage by getting away to an untouched beach area along one of Australia's coasts. The two are so preoccupied with their individual misery that they become quite the careless couple, nearly rear-ending another car, hitting and killing a wandering kangaroo, and accidentally starting a brush fire by neglecting to put out a match properly. Once they arrive at their location (cutting a path through much dense forest in the process), their carelessness continues, eventually causing the wildlife to revolt…

The above synopsis is the one generally used for **LONG WEEKEND** and it's surprisingly deceptive. We are led to believe that the crux of the story is about nature revolting against man and his destructive ways, but upon closer examination, it seems that there's far more going on than that. Re-watching the film for this review, I realize how little it actually has to do with the situation. Clearly, writer Everett De Roche (whose impressive list of Ozploitation credits includes **PATRICK** [1978], **ROAD GAMES** [1981], and the giant-boar **JAWS** [1975] remake **RAZORBACK** (1984)[2]—essential viewing all) had something far deeper and more psychological on his mind, and this is something that director Colin Eggleston was able to capture and con-

2   See *Monster! Digest #2*, p.15

Melissa (Anessa Ramsey) gets so much more than she bargained for when she follows the **YELLOWBRICKROAD**

Their Crime was against nature

nature found them guilty.

LONG ⓂWEEKEND**

STARRING
JOHN HARGREAVES   BRIONY BEHETS

Dugong Films present
LONG WEEKEND
With assistance from
Australian Film Commission
and the
Victorian Film Corporation.

Producer /Director Colin Eggleston
Director of Photography Vincent Monton
Written by Everett De Roche
Music by Michael Carlos
Executive Producer Richard Brennan
Hoyts Distribution

but it also seems apparent that their feelings and actions are brought about by a good deal of guilt. For instance, Marcia comes upon an Eagle's egg that she initially clutches by her side (there's some unsubtle symbolism for you), but ultimately smashes it against a tree in a fit of anger (where it appears that blood spurts from it along with yolk), causing Peter to exclaim, "Why did you do that? It was a living thing!" As the film progresses, it is further suggested that much (if not all) of what we are seeing may not actually be occurring. The most blatant examples of this are the scenes with the manatee (sea cow). Initially thought to be a shark in the ocean, Peter shoots at it, only for Marcia to discover it (and what it really was) later washed up on the beach. He buries the carcass, only for it to somehow keep reappearing (and all the while Marcia hearing the sad cries of its orphaned offspring, or so we're led to believe). Later on, Peter returns to his tent to find his dog suddenly angry and growling. Upon closer examination, he (and we) realizes that this isn't his dog. Whose dog is it and where did it come from? The scene is one and done with no explanation whatsoever. Some animal attacks do appear to be more certain than others, but the film's ambiguity keeps us constantly wondering. This after all, is essentially a two-player piece, and everything that we see onscreen comes from their point of view. There is no third party involved to help make sense of this. *We* the audience are the third party, and it becomes increasingly clear that our pair of protagonists may not be of sound mind. In addition to the animals, we experience (through one or both of them) further unexplained phenomena like a children's play set in the middle of nowhere, a doll that gets washed up on the shore, and (in arguably the film's creepiest moment) the discovery of a submerged van containing a drowned child. Mere symbolism or the visions of a tortured couple…or both? These things are largely left to interpretation, and the film is all the richer and more terrifying and disturbing because of it.

Our leads in this two-player presentation both give remarkable performances. As the hateful and disturbed Marcia, Briony Behets (who was married at the time to director Eggleston) acts up a storm while still maintain-

vey brilliantly. Our thoughtless, unhappy and unlikable couple had recently gone through a traumatic abortion (which we learn of about one-third of the way in) and this appears to be the crux of their shared unhappiness. It has affected Marcia to the point where she is now frigid and unable to have any sort of physical relationship with her husband; she spends much of her time reading romance novels while masturbating to them. Peter, in turn, without a sexual outlet, spends his time either randomly shooting his rifle in the woods and chopping down trees for no particular reason, or, when in a calmer state, quietly surfing along the coast. Yes, these two self-absorbed head-cases are most certainly the villains of the film, and each in turn do things that are reprehensible,

Marcia (Briony Behets) might look relaxed right now, but she's got an unnervingly **LONG WEEKEND** ahead of her...

THE DEVIL'S NIGHTMARE Anglo export pressbook

ing the necessary subtlety that the role calls for. Coming off as utterly annoying and grating in the early scenes (to the point where we actually feel some measure of sympathy for Peter), her character becomes more complicated once we learn why she's acting so cold and bitter. We still don't like the character, but we come to understand her a bit better (or at least as much as the narrative allows for). John Hargreaves' performance as Peter may be even more remarkable, since the aloof character demands that the actor remain quiet and distant, yet still compelling. Hargreaves plays Peter as though he's always in a state of contemplation; at first lost in his own boorish and destructive selfishness before ultimately just trying to get a grip of things as they unfold before him. Ultimately, his character appears to be both the more arrogant *and* tortured of the two (and that's saying something).

Released on DVD and Blu-ray by Synapse in a gorgeous print with both formats carrying the same extras (audio commentary with producer Richard Brennan and director of photography Vincent Monton along with a still gallery accompanied by narration by star Hargreaves and the original trailer), **LONG WEEKEND** is a masterpiece that has only recently begun to receive the attention it so demands.[3] If you haven't seen this one yet, move it immediately to the top of your priority list.

1978, AUSTRALIA. D: COLIN EGGLESTON
AVAILABLE FROM SYNAPSE

---

3   The film was remade in 2008 (from De Roche's screenplay) by **URBAN LEGEND** (1998) director Jamie Blanks, starring Jim Caviezel and Claudia Karvan (a.k.a. **NATURE'S GRAVE** on home video)...but see the original first! *–ed.*

THE DEVIL'S NIGHTMARE

(*La plus longue nuit du diable*; a.k.a. **THE DEVIL WALKS AT MIDNIGHT**, a.k.a. **SUCCUBUS**, a.k.a. **VAMPIRE PLAYGIRLS**)

Reviewed by Steve Fenton

During the 1945 Allied bombing of Berlin (detailed in a black-and-white prologue sequence), a pregnant woman goes into labour, intercut with period combat newsreel footage. The Nazi father, Baron von Rumberg (Jean Servais) hopes for a boy in order to extend his lineage and avoid a longstanding malediction that bodes disaster if a female is born into the accursed clan. The child, expectedly, turns out to be female, so the Baron reluctantly if methodically kills her with his bayonet. This scene is all the more vicious for its insistence on showing the dead infant (even if it is only a peacefully sleeping newborn extra "impaled" on a prop blade through a bloody pillow). The scene thus nastily set, we then proceed into the narrative proper...

Scene shifts ahead—now printed on color stock—to the present day (*circa* 1971) in the chateau of the former fascist father who had committed infanticide decades before. On the grounds of the Von Rumberg estate a woman is brutally murdered while a busload of tourists is *en route*. On the road, the travellers encounter a creepy-looking figure (played by anti-photogenic Fellini

Another scintillating page from **THE DEVIL'S NIGHTMARE**'s Anglo export pressbook

alumnus Daniel Emilfork), looking gauntly reminiscent of Max "Count Orloff" Shreck in F.W. Murnau's silent Expressionist vampire classic **NOSFERATU** (*Nosferatu, eine Symphonie des Grauens*, 1922). Further ominously foreboding events follow. "The *succubus* has come back to the castle!" declares a superstitious villager as he spies the alleged Mark of the Devil on the body of the dead woman found upon the castle grounds. Just as the newcomers arrive, a second woman is almost felled by a fragment of a stone gargoyle face which seemingly spontaneously dislodges itself and topples from the forbidding façade of the Von Rumberg chateau, and this detail makes for a highly effective and evocative piece of visual foreshadowing indeed, implying that supernatural forces may well be (and indeed *are*, as it happens) at work here.

A stern butler with a demeanour not unlike debonair cad's cad George Saunders explains to a young priest that, in 1575 Erika von Rumberg had knifed a monk while he was in the process of exorcizing her. This leads into an explanation of the lasting family curse, which involves the reappearance of a seductive, malignant succubus, as per a long-standing prophecy/curse. It also explains why the Baron had murdered his own newborn daughter years prior.

The guests seek shelter from the familiar raging thunderstorm requisite to this sort of *gothique*. The smokily sultry Erika Blanc (who at this point in her career was frequenting import sexploitation like Cesare Canevari's **A MAN FOR EMMANUELLE** [*Io, Emmanuelle* / *"I,*

Emmanuelle", 1969]) shortly materializes to ooze sultry looks at all the other castle guests (of both genders). As a result we are treated to sundry close-ups—in true Italo *giallo* fashion—of cast members' guilty/furtive/covetous/selfish eyes. The starchy butler babbles on about the existence of the fabled succubus: a foul demoness of temptation bent on enticing weak-willed mortals to eternal Hellfire and Damnation via appealing to their basest bodily lusts.

Technical advisor on **THE DEVIL'S NIGHTMARE** (1971) was André Hunebelle (spearhead of the fantabulously fab '60s *Fantômas* trilogy, starring Jean Marais in the title role), which might explain some of the present film's lush visual detailing and dense atmosphere. Jean-Baptiste Brismée commands laudable directorial control of all the various components of the drama, and André Goeffer's cinematography is assured, full and eye-catching. Very much in the vein—if by no means the camped-up style—of William Castle's otherwise entirely non-connected **HOUSE ON HAUNTED HILL** (1959), shortly after their arrival the guests discover to their alarm that they are inescapably sealed inside the chateau. Seemingly boding further ill for the forcibly detained "guests", the ceiling "bleeds" on one of the visitors. It turns out that, as well as dabbling in such dark occult arts and sciences as alchemy, Baron von Rumberg keeps a well-stocked collection of still-operable in-house medieval torture implements; therefore being pegged as the most obvious (and therefore least likely, if you know your whodunit tropes) suspect in the local homicides.

The dreaded succubus (which not unsurprisingly turns out to be the succulent Ms. Blanc, natch; it was obvious right from the first sight of her) soon inspires the other cast members to bring about their own demises through enactment of the big seven deadly no-nos: including Gluttony, Adultery, Avarice, etc. Her victims are all killed whilst in a state of Mortal Sin. While a victim chokes on a lavish feast of wine and lobster (committing "Gluttony"), Blanc's supernatural visage changes fluidly to a chillingly frigid, grey-skinned hag's (no Heimlich manoeuvre performed here!). This transformative image, despite its utter simplicity of execution—achieved through special color filters, altered lighting and only a bare minimum of makeup—freezes the blood far more effectively than any overdone new millennial prosthetic or CGI bogeyman (or bogey*woman*, for that matter) ever could; and that includes all those Asiatic long-haired ghost chicks seen in umpteen **RINGU** clones. This whole scene in **THE DEVIL'S NIGHTMARE** recalls the similar one in Riccardo Freda's **I VAMPIRI** (*"The Vampires"*, a.k.a. **THE DEVIL'S COMMANDMENT**, 1959), wherein Gianna Maria Canale's character deteriorates from an alluringly vampish starlet to a wizened crone in the space of a few frames.

The deaths in the vicinity of the Von Rumberg place continue. One woman expires when she is swallowed up into a shimmering heap of powdered gold ("Avarice"). Another joint murder sees the succubus beheading a man by guillotine and shutting his girlfriend inside a handy iron maiden (requisite Gothic torture/murder devices both). Overall, a satisfyingly dark mood is instilled, despite the typical carelessly-done English redubbing job.

Bringing into play some of the more pronounced religious/anticlerical symbolism—replete with mandatory phallic Eve/Eden innuendo—a female victim is threatened by a large serpent transformed from a stick. Blanc seeks to tantalize the unswayably pious priestly hero (Jacques Monseau), who tries to put an end to all the Satanic shenanigans. (**SPOILER ALERT!**) Finally, the young padre forges a tentative bargain with the Devil himself in order to save the souls of all the recent victims that Blanc's character has sent hurtling into purgatory awaiting their final judgment. (Interestingly enough, this act of self-sacrifice by a clergyman actually prefigures the title character's final redemptive act in William Friedkin's **THE EXORCIST** [1973].)

The film's twist ending seems all the more bogus after the shameless overkill of such technique in the 1980s/1990s and beyond, but here somehow suits the film's old-world, often expressionistic tone. A lot of people would probably bad-mouth a film like **THE DEVIL'S NIGHTMARE**, but don't you believe them. It's a definite must-see of Euro horrotica, and of the highest order for fans of the form.

Back in the '80s and '90s, this movie was extant on Beta/VHS cassette from all sorts of budget video labels. I viewed two differing prints of it, and both were of far-from-pristine quality. It was formerly available—

and still might be, if you're the type who likes to scour yard sales and thrift stores in search of "retro" bargains in obsolescent formats—on Interglobal (a notoriously shoddy Toronto-based operation, now justifiably long-out-of-business). Besides being duped at the unsatisfactory, cost-cutting LP ("long-play") recording speed, their tape—released as **THE DEVIL WALKS AT MIDNIGHT**—seemed to be missing some scenes, or else its continuity had been shuffled somewhere along the line, and any nudity was missing from the video transfer (possibly indicating it was an old censored TV print?). Another version (erstwhile extant on Applause Video tapes) was reputedly "uncut", albeit bearing the crudely spliced video-generated **SUCCUBUS** retitle, which may well have fooled some rank amateurs into believing it was Jesús Franco's **NECRONOMICON – GETRÄUMTE SÜNDEN** (1968) under its US theatrical release title. **THE DEVIL'S NIGHTMARE** was also formerly available on at least three other domestic home video labels (i.e., Monterey, Saturn Productions and Regal Video), none of which I ever saw so can't comment on them, although Regal's version (likewise entitled **THE DEVIL WALKS AT MIDNIGHT**) came with some real nifty cover art, though it might feasibly (?) have been struck from the same choppy source print as the crummy aforementioned Interglobal version.

1971, BELGIUM/ITALY.
D: JEAN-BAPTISTE BRISMÉE
AVAILABLE FROM REDEMPTION/IMAGE

THE DEVIL'S NIGHTMARE French tie-in novel

JERSEY SHORE SHARK ATTACK

Reviewed by Christos Mouroukis

Ad-lines: "Your worst fears will surface." "Your Worst Fears Will Service."

Fans often say that filmmakers *"don't make them like this anymore"*, and although it is true that nothing as wild as the 1960s or as provocative as the 1970s will ever come back, I see the producers' tactics as being somewhat similar, even though the geographical landscape is ever changing. Case in point: the rip-offs (or as they are often called today, "mockbusters"). The 1980s were indeed a golden era when the Italians made all our favourite post-apocalypse epics (or any other genre, for that matter) "based" on the ones their Hollywood contemporaries were making[4], but was that any different from what say, The Asylum often does nowadays? Sure, it is sad that the governments' Film Councils in Europe killed genre film and replaced it with an irrelevant and failed point-checking art-house "business" model, but instead of crying over this harsh truth, why don't we cherish what we have?

This film under review here is not exactly a "rip-off", but its title was "inspired" (insert: in order to cash in) by MTV's widely successful *Jersey Shore* TV show (2009-2012). The unfortunate thing for this Fred Olen Ray-produced[5] film is that it premiered on SyFy in June 2012 while the MTV show had its last episode aired in December of the same year, which says a lot about its popularity at the time. It is easy for TV shows to make fun of films

---

4   By the way, I have noticed that everybody is calling Bruno Mattei a copycat director; although this is not false, I have to ask: Who wasn't back then?

5   Fred Olen Ray produced this with Griff Furst, Kimberly A. Ray, and Peter Sullivan.

and remain contemporary, but movies—even TV movies—can't rush as much in order to remain *that* current.

Other than the title, this film was directed John Shepphird (it is his last film to date) very much in the MTV style, what with title cards of the main characters' names and funky editing (by Randy Carter). As you can imagine, the cast consists of young people with hot bodies, but no matter how pleasant they are on the eye, they also come across as a bit annoying (the writing doesn't help either because everybody speaks as if they are the same person, so much so that I had a hard time telling who is who), but luckily for us they are rounded by some seasoned pros (Tony Sirico and Paul Sorvino are good examples of actors who are above such things, yet they are here, and they deliver) that much to their credit try to save the day.

The titular menace is actually interesting: a bunch of albino bull sharks with white skin and red eyes (insert a pot joke here) that react to vibration. There is some grey and under-the-table construction going on at the Jersey Shore and that is what brought the fish there; angry as they are, they spend a good time of the picture massacring the swimmers.

A few years ago someone asked me, *"Why don't you get a job in TV?"* I worked on small-time television several times, but I wasn't when this question came about. There were several reasons for that, but the short answer (and the one I gave) was, *"Because I don't like TV"*. To which the person I was talking to replied *"Oh, I like TV"*. I will never forget how peculiar this moment seemed to my brain. I wonder, who likes TV, and why? The news broadcasts are controlled by mega-corporations with ties to this or that political party and are dictated by economic interests. The commercials do bore people to death. The sports are corrupt and pre-arranged. The talk-shows are for idiots. Etc. Then I thought, *"Is there anything about TV that I like?"* Yeah, I watch the occasional Marvel TV series (*Agents of S.H.I.E.L.D.* [2013-], *Agent Carter* [2015-], or *Daredevil* [2015-]), but mostly, I don't miss the SyFy monster movies. For those two reasons alone, television in 2015 is still relevant to me.

2012, USA. D: JOHN SHEPPHIRD
AVAILABLE FROM ANCHOR BAY

MILFS VS. ZOMBIES

Reviewed by Brian Harris

A zombie apocalypse may be underway, but that doesn't stop four housewives from getting together for some drinks and bonding. That is, until their husbands arrive to save the day with a flesh-eating horde in tow. New plan: head to the children's camp and save the kids. And, other stuff happens. Lots and lots of other stuff.

If I didn't know better, I would have sworn this Z-budget production had been made during the mid-2Ks, when

Oh my friggin' gawd! It's a **JERSEY SHORE SHARK ATTACK**!

Actress Ophelia Rain can't escape this horny zombie!

pretty much everything made it onto disc and into stores. There I sat, remote in hand, turning the volume up and down in a futile attempt to alleviate the effects of the awful sound quality on my television's speakers. This didn't bode well for me; **MILFS VS. ZOMBIES'** (2015) runtime was a whopping 105 minutes! You know you're in for a rough ride when you catch yourself constantly checking the time to see how much longer until the final credits scroll. I made it about 48 minutes in before nearly calling it quits. Thankfully, some liquid courage helped me along…and I don't say that in jest.

MILFS VS. ZOMBIES is an exercise in patience; one to which I will never subject myself to again. After shutting down *WildsideCinema.com*, I assumed I'd never come across mind-numbing cinema like this again, but fate can be a cruel mistress indeed. If I could sum this film up with a few words it would be, "third-rate Troma". Some might feel that's a compliment. It isn't.

But, there's nudity! And zombie rape! True, some of the nudity was impressive, but most of it was just grungy, and the rape was beyond unnecessary.

The "high school kids turned aspiring horror filmmakers" of the '00s were able to serve up healthy doses of jank A/V quality, a few farts jokes, the occasional blown-out beaver and some corn syrup blood with varying degrees of indie success. Companies clamored to acquire as much as they could, expecting to snag the Next Big Thing from the Next Big Horror Filmmaker. They'd dump dozens of Z-grade productions to disc on a weekly basis, eventually choking the life out of the market. Most of it wasn't hipster "bad" either—we're talking just plain bad. Guaranteed, **MILFS VS. ZOMBIES** would have ended up in one of those giant "Going out of Business" 75% off piles, had it been from that era.

Director Twigg failed to demand more from his actors, as many seemed to have barely memorized their lines. They were either way over-the-top and fumbling or phoning it in completely. Now, I can forgive amateur actors—even haunted house actors need to make a buck—but this crowd was especially awkward and downright intolerable. The only enjoyable character to be found was James Balsamo's clownish Tom… because everybody has at least one friend like *that*. I still cringed my way through most of the film, though. Not even the mad-libbed cameo from Troma's Lloyd Kaufman was able to raise this steamer to passable.

Why in the hell did this need Shawn C. Phillips exactly?

Special effects were uneven, going from grade-school Halloween pageant caliber to mildly impressive throughout the runtime. When it worked, it worked, but consistency was sorely lacking. As mentioned previously, the sound was harsh. The lighting and cinematography were uninspired but tolerable. It was "light, point, shoot"…and it all added up to a visually boring production.

The story, what little there was, was positively dreadful. Writers Leslie Monk and Juan Sanchez should pass on taking a bow for this mess; I've seen children utilize better storytelling. The dialogue was stiff and clunky, only managing to work when it was catering to the lowest common denom. As I sat wondering when it would all come to an end, *KABOOM*, it does…with the kind of finale one might expect from inept writers with no clear vision. If they were shooting for something akin a no-budget "*Desperate Housewives* meets *The Walking Dead*," they failed.

"But wouldn't it be cool if the MILFs carried wine bottles, frying pans, rolling pins and kitchen butcher knives as zombie-killing weapons?" No, not really.

Mexican pressbook ad

Brad Twigg takes credit for editing, so on top of sloppy direction he also drops the ball on the editing front. **MILFS VS. ZOMBIES** was way too long at 105 minutes; it felt like an insanely padded, unfinished short that would never end. Sequence after unrelated juvenile sequence was tacked-on to extend the runtime when less should have been more. With a tighter story, they could have pared this thing down to 93 minutes. Though, in my opinion, even that would have been too long.

MILFS VS. ZOMBIES is a skeevy little film that brings nothing to the table, and this is coming from an exploitation cinema fan. I'm all about socially unacceptable, artistically irredeemable cinema, but even I know when I'm watching a turd. *Hey, dirtbags have standards too.* I'm sure this will do well with Twigg's friends and family, and there's no doubt a few less-than-demanding online devotees that will be willing to give this a glowing review. But I cannot recommend anyone purchase a film that I was barely able to sit through.

2015, USA. DIRECTOR: BRAD TWIGG
AVAILABLE FROM FUZZY MONKEY FILMS

MUSEO DEL HORROR

("Museum of Horror")

Reviewed by Steve Fenton

Over the years, I've gotten so sick of hearing about how inferior Mexican horror films supposedly are when compared to just about everything else, and people moaning that Euro films (etc.) are way better on the whole. I'm sure Tim P. (who I reckon is as much of a Mexi-movie buff as I am) might have much the same to say in regards to naysayers about his ongoing passion for Indian fantasy cinema, a form which has still to "catch" on in any sort of big way with cult movie mavens here in the West; although Mexploitation movies now have a sizeable and ever-growing following the world over, I'm glad—yet at the same time somewhat sad—to say. But I bet half those who dis Mexican genre films are just making snap judgements on films they probably haven't even *heard* of yet, let alone actually seen, such is their built-in bias. Hell, I love Continental horrors as much as the next guy (or gal), yet to me the best Mexico has to offer can easily stand proudly shoulder-to-shoulder alongside Europe's finest genre efforts; no ifs, ands or buts about it. So sue me!

I'd defy anyone to say that the introductory passage which unrolls behind the credits to **MUSEO DEL HORROR** (1964) is not every bit as stylish and competently executed as anything conceived by Italian horror maestro Mario Bava: there is an excess of sinister, mist-soaked atmosphere and the chiaroscuro lighting and camerawork are great, even if the content is admittedly several points shy of innovative, or even particularly fresh; but then the same might be said about many of the Euro examples that the fanboys routinely gush all over, so we'll say no more about it.

A late-night street scene: strategically placed lighting reflects off drifting fog as a lone young woman hurries along the sidewalk of a darkened and otherwise deserted street, her heels clacking on the flagstones. From the pregnant stygian blackness of the surrounding shadows, a black-draped, stealthily prowling figure in slouch hat and cloak observes her from concealment a short distance away, follows her, then rushes out to scare her out of her wits with his (its?) ugly, grossly-deformed countenance. This horrid apparition then proceeds to carry the swooned victim off to its cemetery hideout, which lies below a hidden entrance in a grave within concealed chambers. The shrouded figure lays out its helpless female captive on a tabletop, and then promptly pours a cauldron of (supposedly) scorching hot wax over her tormented features as she shrieks in agony…

A promising start, you may well think, and you'd be right. The foregoing really primes you for what is still to come, and the film's gloomy, doomy demeanour is consistently maintained throughout.

The initial minutes of this extended mood-establishing opener invoke memories of *Signor* Bava's wonderful **BARON BLOOD** (*Gli orrori del castello di Norimberga / "The Horrors of Nuremberg Castle"*, 1972), which in turn borrowed heavily from André de Toth's 3-D Vincent Pricer **HOUSE OF WAX** (1953), of which **MUSEO** is a veritable carbon copy story-wise (and sometimes stylistically, as well). Even though that cinematic form was only just getting started in Italy at the time, the film contains classical *giallo* ingredients, but simultaneously makes no bones about also imitating the '53 American film (there's also a lot of *krimi* in it too, à la one of the numerous Edgar Wallace mystery series being produced in West Germany during the same general period). Director Baledón is here captured at his moodiest and most melancholy since his somberly melancholic Jekyll/Hyde variation **THE MAN AND THE MONSTER** (*El hombre y el monstruo*, 1959), and generously layers on the dark, forbiddingly oppressive ambience with zero procrastination right from frame one.

The charismatic, prolific and long-lived Joaquín Cordero (1923-2013) here makes a return to the Mexi-horror genre (on top of **THE HELL OF FRANKENSTEIN** [*Orlak, el infierno de Frankenstein*, 1960] and playing the lead villain in both *Dr. Satan* films, he also appeared in the Baledónian werewolf-woman flick **LA LOBA** [*"The She-Wolf"*, 1965]). **MUSEO** sees him enacting the equivalent of Vincent Price's **HOUSE OF WAX** role, only instead of riding around in a wheelchair to give himself an air of pathos, Cordero limps around on a cane.

Ignore the derivative nature of it all. What's strangely refreshing about this film is its complete unselfconsciousness about ripping-off its fun-if-overrated Yankee predecessor, while at the same time doing a creditable job of infusing the material with its own distinct ethnic style. There are shameless touches of *grand guignol*, such as severed human heads pickled in jars of formaldehyde— at a bona fide hospital, yet!—as well as all the usual "red herrings", like a suspicious-looking taxidermist, and also a pair of Burke and Hare-inspired body-snatchers (one of whom is played by Mexploitation "ugly" Vicente Lara, alias "Cacama", who, due to his fuzzy facial hair, was cast as pseudo-wolfmen more than once [e.g., in Gilberto Martínez Solares' **SANTO AND BLUE DEMON AGAINST THE MONSTERS** {*Santo el enmascarado de plata y Blue Demon contra los monstruos*, 1970}]).

HOUSE OF WAX's Folies Bergère-style dance numbers are here replaced with the mandatory musical interludes that slow down the above-cited **ORLAK** and many other otherwise perfectly respectable Mexican horror movies. However, the present film succeeds in being far less whimsical and corny overall than **HOUSE**, with a dark tone all its own. I prefer to think of **MUSEO** as more of an *homage* to **HOUSE** (by way of Michael Curtiz's original version **MYSTERY OF THE WAX MUSEUM** [1933]) rather than merely a rip-off of it. Perhaps the fact that its main inspiration source had been shot not just in Technicolor but in 3-D too—while **MUSEO** was filmed only in flat, two-dimensional (if by no means lifeless) B&W—might have a good deal to do with the different mood attained, which sufficiently distinguishes it from its better-known Hollywood counterpart; in fact, their differences/similarities might make the two films an ideal double-bill (with **MUSEO** as the second feature, natch).

As is usual with Baledón, the more mundane scenes and box office-required "lovey-dovey" stuff between the heroine and her male admirers tend to put a damper on the action, but are all par for the course in an old-school melodrama such as this. When the wholesome heroine Marta (Patricia Condé) visits the bitter Cordero's sculpture studio, "sexual tension" between the two runs high, so he forcefully grabs her and plants a firm kiss on her lips, then we "tastefully" segue into another love song chirped by that ostrich-feathered cleavage-queen with the fur boa at the nightclub. Numerous subplots are wo-

Mexican lobby card

Mexican horror movie **MUSEO DEL HORROR** is a literal carbon-copy of the American horror film **HOUSE OF WAX**, a fact which is most apparent in the progression of the story.

ven in and out of each other, and it's difficult to ascertain whether they are intended to come together at some later point, or not. They do eventually (well, *kind of*, anyway).

The young doctor at the hospital (Julio Alemán) has got the major hots for the heroine (he's also got a shelf full of pickled heads), and on the side employs the services of the aforementioned body-snatchers to provide him with (what else?) bodies for whatever ungodly experiments are up his sleeve. Such activities mark him as a potential suspect in all the murders, of course, and, however fishy he might smell, seldom has a more obvious red herring been waved under our noses, so we ain't falling for it. Elsewhere, an equally obvious prostitute (you can tell this by the brazen way she flaunts her hefty hind-end as she walks) meets the disfigured murderer on a foggy street, where she unwisely approaches him to request a light for her cigarette, having as-yet not seen his horrifying visage. True to form, having spirited her off to his graveyard "workshop", the monster there douses his newest "acquisition" with scalding wax and adds her to his collection.

Here sporting a bushy mustache, which somewhat diminishes his usual quite-strong resemblance to disgraced ex-US prez Richard "Tricky Dickie" Nixon, David Reynoso plays the staunch representative of law and order on the case. Subplots involving busy detectives investigating the murders (some committed with poison darts) are woven in among the many red herrings, but the lack of English dialogue makes it awkward for non-Spanish-speaking viewers like me to decipher subtleties without subtitles. I don't doubt that a fan-subbed version of this film exists somewhere (on Cinemageddon, where I'm not and don't want to be a member, perhaps?), but if so, I've yet to see a copy with English translation.

As is common in Baledón's work, much (in this case, *all*) of the action takes place either in twilight or at night, meaning that he can pile on the shadow and creative lighting effects like there's no tomorrow; which apparently there *isn't* in this film of seemingly everlasting nighttime. Its very milieu proves that the director was truly dedicated to his craft, as setting an entire narrative after dark requires a good deal more creativity in order to sustain not just the desired mood, but also from a more technical standpoint (proper lighting of course being one of the main concerns). There are no fraudulent day-for-night scenes here!

After those ruthless grave-robbers kill a cemetery night watchman then coldly and methodically bury him in an open grave, at around the 40-minute mark we ease into a truly nightmarish sequence wherein the dead rise from their graves as cobweb-shrouded, quiet-faced somnambulists. This all turns out to be a fevered dream of the heroine's (a foreshadowing of the inevitable horror to come?). At the time when I first laid eyes on **MUSEO DEL HORROR** back in about 1990 or so I had no idea where the preceding described sequence originated—it was unlike anything else I'd ever seen in a Mexi-horror up until that point—although at the time I rightly assumed it wasn't originally shot for this film (the scene has a similar eerily haunting quality to the fleeting glimpses of the winged daemon in above-average horror stylist Miguel Morayta's **DOCTOR SATÁN** [1966]). Not to belittle Baledón's own input and considerable creative chops, but this inserted scene's entire construction looks to have been overseen by someone else (indeed it was!); someone with a decided eye for the "look" of nightmare, though with a distinctly different style. And here comes another, much more direct and overt Mario Bava connection: you see, said passage (albeit in color) had actually originated in Bava's sumptuous gothic horror peplum **HERCULES IN THE HAUNTED WORLD** (*Ercole al centro della Terra*, a.k.a. **HERCULES AT THE CENTER OF THE EARTH**, 1961), starring Christopher Lee, from a scary scene close to the end of that film when heroic Herc (Reg Park) is menaced by a bunch of ghostly witch-demons. Hence, considering all **MUSEO**'s other Bavian touches, although one can't help but wonder whether the brief (roughly 30-second) excerpt was used with or without official permission, it's nonetheless rather appropriate that it was reused by Baledón here. However, seeing the Italo maestro's originally color footage rendered in flat B&W is rather disorienting, although it still looks just as eerie. Incidentally, the same footage, this time printed in its original color, later reappeared in Gilberto Martínez Solares' Santo/Blue Demon opus **LAND OF THE DEAD** (*El mundo de los muertos*, a.k.a. **THE WORLD OF THE DEAD**, 1970).

As **MUSEO** builds, Baledón's reliance on reshooting each "monster" scene much the same as the preceding one, as if to some carefully drawn-out blueprint, grows a mite repetitive: the same rapid zoom into Ugly's puffy, rubbery face is repeated at least twice more after its first introduction. A rather episodic and predictable "rhythm" begins to develop.

When one of the kidnapped girls escapes within the fiend's underground hideout however, while she goes into hysterics at the sight of them we get rapidly-cut "shock close-ups" of sundry scary cadavers whose faces resemble nothing so much as emaciated (zombie?) Cabbage Patch Kids! Tacky, for sure—but every rose has its thorn, as the old saying goes. At least they snap you out of any lethargy that steals over you during the film's numerous incomprehensible talkathons, but such gimmicky bits bring to mind celebrated Horrorwood schloxploitationeer William Castle at his absolute schlockiest (*à la* his Theremin-drenched haunted house spook-show **13 GHOSTS** [1960], which thankfully bears little or no resemblance to that pointless New Millennial "reboot" of the same name).

Now, might the killer be the grave-robber-employing medico or that secretive animal-stuffer? This taxidermist too keeps a rotted human noggin in a jar on his desk (I guess they were kinda like the "Pet Rocks" of turn-of-the-last-century Mexico), so he's definitely a candidate for perp. But I won't be spoiling a thing (you know it right from the get-go, anyway) if I tell you who the culprit is…like Vinnie Price's quest for his perfect Joan of

Top: DVD cover for the Mexican release of **MUSEO DEL HORROR** (*sans* any English subtitles). **Middle and above:** glimpses of the gruesome bits that pop up in this classic Mexican horror flick.

Arc in **WAX** '53, Cordero too has an "ideal woman"—a certain headless wax figure in his museum that's just aching for the right topper as its finishing touch. Gee, whose noggin *could* it be, we wonder…? Another girl gets nabbed by the fedora'd freak, and her head thereafter "mysteriously" turns up on Cordero's star dummy. When the heroine shows up, she identifies the head on the wax figure as resembling a missing girlfriend, then Cordero begins to act…um…*odd*. The suspect doc and taxidermist are questioned by the cops about any potential involvement in the abduction murders. Of course, while they're wasting time fishing for red herrings, wild-eyed Cordero begins to show his more obsessive, verging-on-dementia side to the coquettish heroine. He shortly snaps outright and drags her in the general direction of his busy workshop, intending to give her the full-body wax treatment. Needless to say, the hero arrives in the proverbial nick of time in order to rescue the struggling heroine before she can be doused with the hot goop and turned into a statue (ironically enough to live forever in death).

Many Mexican movies were derivative of US sources, but seldom more obviously than here. **MUSEO DEL HORROR** is a literal carbon-copy of **HOUSE OF WAX**, a fact which is most apparent in the progression of the story more so than in the actual mood attained and mostly sustained (in that area, the two films are worlds apart). Whereas **HOUSE** had been a colorful, oftentimes brightly lit and rather too-quaint affair, albeit at times given visceral impact by some pretty macabre passages, **MUSEO** is a dark, sullen and despairing film within whose every shadowy recess lurks sinister intent.

In spite of a few traditionally schlocky episodes, Baledón's film succeeds in for the most part being far more visually arresting than de Toth's multi-hued horror extravaganza (which was basically only extant in order to exploit the roughly year-long early-'50s 3-D craze: remember that gratuitously overlong scene of the guy repeatedly bapping his paddleball directly into the camera *ad nauseam*?). **MUSEO** ably illustrates just how adept Rafael Baledón really was at creating brooding atmosphere when he really applied himself to the task at hand. The film must stand as his visual masterpiece within the horror genre, and it is many times more memorable than its inspiration source.

1964, MEXICO. D: RAFAEL BALEDÓN
AVAILABLE FROM TELEVISA

SICK GIRL

Reviewed By L. Thomas Tripp

In honor of Halloween, I decided to take some friendly advice and watch **SICK GIRL** (2007), which was written and directed by Eben McGarr, someone I was previously unfamiliar with. Happily, the film was no disappointment, and I found myself enthralled by the viewing experience. This film seemed to dish out comedy and cruelty in perfectly proportional amounts—much to my entertainment.

This grotesque roller coaster ride begins with a school bus traveling down a primarily deserted road somewhere in rural America. The bus stops to pick up Izzy (Leslie Andrews), a crazy hitchhiker looking for a ride and some trouble. Meanwhile, two schoolgirls toss a pair of panties out the window for two boys following the bus in a car. Be-

There seem to be some subtle indications that Izzy (Leslie Andrews) might be a very **SICK GIRL**

fore the credits even begin, Izzy attacks a nun on the bus, so they pull over, throw her out, and drive away quickly.

As the credits roll, Izzy meets the two boys trying to track the girls on the bus, and they act like a couple of chauvinistic pigs looking for a good time. Things quickly get out of control as Izzy brutally attacks both of the teenage scumbags, leaving one as a hostage. After stealing their car—and a gun inside the glove compartment—Izzy departs to find the bus and finish the job, which she does in brutal fashion.

Izzy returns home to the farm, and she sees Kevin (Charlie Trepany), her little brother, receiving fighting lessons from Barney (Eben's brother John McGarr), a family friend. She learns that Kevin is getting bullied at school, but he is unwilling to explain the situation to Izzy, denoting his uneasiness towards his sister. At this point, it is apparent that Izzy is her brother's legal guardian, and with no parents around, the brunt of raising him falls on Izzy and Rusty (Chris W. King), the older brother, but he is away in the military. A series of flashback scenes depict a complicated relationship between Izzy and Rusty; however, Izzy does have a primarily good relationship with Kevin, and she treats him like a son.

Kevin goes to school, but a trio of bullies continues to badger him. Before things get out of hand, Izzy arrives to break up the ruckus, and the ruffians flee. She sends Kevin home so she can go after the three bullies. A whirlwind of calamity is about to be unleashed, which culminates when Izzy captures and tortures Kevin's tormentors, taking the ringleader hostage.

Barney and Kevin have no idea what Izzy is doing with her free time, but she begins to show signs of mental distress. As Christmas comes, Izzy, Kevin and Barney exchange gifts. Much to Barney's surprise, Izzy gives her little brother a gun, yet he is only nine years old. Barney, once a friend to her father, lectures her about the inappropriate gift to no avail.

Things take a turn for the worst as Izzy returns to her barn—a makeshift torture shack—only to unleash savage brutality upon her three hostages, which includes one of the girls from the bus. Unfortunately, Barney and Kevin find her in the midst of mutilation, only heightening her rage and intensifying her rampage. Izzy must convince her terrified brother that she is sorry; however, that becomes a real challenge as the resolution proceeds. What will become of Izzy and Kevin?

This film was brilliantly grotesque and equally funny. Eben McGarr wrote and directed a fantastic film, which easily filled the genres of comedy, crime, and horror. In addition, Leslie Andrews, John McGarr, and Charlie Trepany performed beautifully. As an added treat, Stephen Geoffreys—who played "Evil" Ed from **FRIGHT NIGHT** (1985)—had a cameo role as meek schoolteacher Mr. Putski. Interestingly, Eben McGarr also produced the film, so it radiated his particular creative vision throughout; thus, the production was purely independent,

The French (Region 2) DVD release of **MUTANT**

which gave the film a uniquely rustic feel—as did the atmosphere of location and use of cinematography.

With all its brutal intensity, this flick was worth its running time, and proved that good films don't have to cost a fortune to make. As a shorter film, the story was not sacrificed one bit, and it moved along nicely. If you haven't watched **SICK GIRL**, be certain that you do, especially if you like being shocked. This film was terrifyingly terrific and suspenseful to the end!

2007, USA. D: EBEN MCGARR
AVAILABLE FROM SYNAPSE FILMS

MUTANT
(a.k.a. **NIGHT SHADOWS**)

Reviewed by Michael Elvidge

Ad Line: "Mankind's Deadliest Threat Will Not Come From The Skies"

I never have seen or heard much about this 1984 "zombie" film **MUTANT**—not to be confused with **MUTANT** (a.k.a. **FORBIDDEN WORLD**, 1982), the **ALIEN** (1979) rip-off—and happened to discover it on DVD only just recently. To warn you in advance, this review may contain some spoilers, but not to the point of ruination.

Let's get started…late at night we see a groundskeeper wander the yard of a mansion; he finds a strange substance on the ground and takes a sample of it. He then investigates the basement of the mansion—actually a

One of the inhuman monstrosities of **MUTANT** challenges you to a zombified stare-down!

rooming house—there he finds a body with a vagina-like slit on the palm of its, hand when suddenly he is done-in by a monster only seen in shadow.

Josh (Wings Hauser) and Mike (Lee Montgomery) Cameron are brothers out on a road trip, driving down a stretch of highway when they swerve and narrowly miss hitting an oncoming pick-up truck. Moments later the truck reappears behind them and starts ramming the back of the brothers' car, loaded with screaming rednecks throwing bottles. The Cameron Boys' convertible drives off the road and ends up down an embankment near a river. Yokels laugh and torment the two and drive off, leaving the brothers to hitchhike to town. An older man named Mel (Stuart Culpepper) gives them a ride and drops them off near the town, yet they still must walk a distance to get to it. He warns them not to go out after dark, but it is night by the time they get to the actual town. A drunk bar patron stumbles past, exiting Jack's Tavern and walking off into the distance, and doesn't respond to the brothers' calls. Mike goes after him, but the drunk is strangled by an unseen monster with burning, steaming hands. Josh follows Mike and they find the drunk dead, his face melted. Mike runs off to get the police, going into Jack's Tavern to use the phone. Some of the bar patrons happen to be the rednecks that road-raged them earlier, and they recognize Mike. Josh enters and tries to stop the confrontation, but it erupts into a rough-and-tumble barroom brawl, only to be broken up by the local Sheriff, Will Stewart (Bo Hopkins). Josh and Mike take the Sheriff to the site of the body only to find a different drunk guy sleeping there. The Sheriff advises them to stay out of trouble, then notices that there is a strange yellow substance near the scene of the missing body; he collects a sample of it and then takes the brothers to the hospital to get the knife wound that Mike received in the melee tended to.

Sheriff Stewart then drives them to the mansion rooming house seen at the start of the film. Mrs. Mapes (Mary Nell Santacroce), the older woman that owns the place shows them to their rooms, giving Josh a crappy-looking room while Mike gets a nice, clean, well-furnished one. Looking out from his second-story window, Josh spies a strange figure walking outside in the yard. Planning to get the car fixed and get out of the town the next day, the two hit the hay. Mike is awakened by something during the night and pulled under the bed as smoke emits from the monstrosity beneath it. The following morning Josh goes to Mike's room but finds he isn't there, and Mrs. Mapes says she hasn't seen him. Josh decides to go into town finding the only business open is Jack's Tavern. A female bartender named Holly (Jody Medford) also hasn't seen Mike and informs Josh that the nearest service station is four or five miles away. Holly, also a school teacher in the small town, offers to take Josh to the service station.

Meanwhile, Sheriff Stewart and Dr. Myra Tate (Jennifer Warren) examine the yellow substance that melted the sample jar taken earlier. It turns out to be blood…but not human. As they discuss this there is a loud noise in the hospital; they find a door leading outside is open and blood has been stolen from a storage fridge.

Josh and Holly stop at the school she teaches at. It's closed for the day but they find a student named Billy (Cary Guffey) sitting in class, who claims his parents have disappeared. Then there is a growling sound from somewhere in the school, which leads Josh and Holly to the basement, where they find the body of a young girl. Redneck leader/school janitor Albert Hogue (Marc Clement), who they tangled with earlier at the Tavern, appears and a swordfight with metal bars commences. Josh escapes, and later when the police arrive, Albert tries to blame the death of the schoolgirl on Josh. Sheriff Stewart allows Dr. Tate to examine the body of the girl before it goes to the coroner.

The Sheriff arrives at the rooming house and finds a man on the floor near death, with gross-looking burns on his face. Moments later, the guy bites the big one. Stewart decides it's time to call in to a higher police authority for backup.

Josh wants to find his brother Mike, but Holly warns him that he is a suspect in the murder of the schoolgirl. He then inexplicably passes out, waking up in the local hospital, where Dr. Tate asks if he touched the body of the girl. He says he did. The Dr. speculates that his fainting may have been a chemical reaction to something on the schoolgirl's body.

When backup arrives at the rooming house, the body that Stewart found has gone missing. Stewart's superior thinks the Sheriff drinks too much and he is not doing his job properly, and if he doesn't resolve all that's going on in the town he'll be suspended. We also learn that some sort of event happened in Stewart's past police work that ended up getting him demoted and sent to the small town to begin with.

Dr. Tate examines the schoolgirl's body as her colleague complains of a flu. Dr. Tate says she'll give him a flu shot after the examination, but he starts to mutate out in the hallway behind the other doctor, changing into a zombie-like creature with pulsating skin and slits on the palms of his hands oozing the yellow substance. Once transformed, he goes after Dr. Tate…

That isn't the entire plot—I truly don't want to tell you anymore of the details, and will just say this: at one point **MUTANT** explodes with zombie horde action. Another thing I'll say: the cause of the zombies in **MUTANT** is not due to the supernatural or the occult. The pace of the film builds slowly to a zombie-filled grand finale. **MUTANT** has sort of a "small town hiding the truth" and partially a "whodunit" component to the plot, and it's not as graphic as you would think when it comes to zombie violence, giving the film a traditional horror movie feel. The makeup is handled very well; the zombies bleed yellow blood, have pulsing flesh, and bluish-grey skin color with black around the eyes. Another trait of the zombies in the film seems to be nocturnal activity, as they are only seen at night.

The first director of **MUTANT**, Marc Rosman, was replaced during filming after the studio disagreed about the way he was shooting the film. He was replaced by movie Renaissance man John "Bud" Cardos, whose career included stunts, acting and directing. He starred in films like **SATAN'S SADISTS** (1969), did stunts in **THE INCREDIBLE 2-HEADED TRANSPLANT** (1971) and directed such films as **KINGDOM OF THE SPIDERS** (1977), **THE DARK** (1979), and **THE DAY TIME ENDED** (1979). Rosman is now known for directing **A CINDERELLA STORY** (2004)

and **THE PERFECT MAN** (2005, USA), but he was also involved in horror earlier in his career, for example **THE HOUSE ON SORORITY ROW** (1983), which he also scripted.

The star of **MUTANT**, Wings Hauser, has over 100 film and television acting credits to his name. He was formerly a football player, but due to a sports injury he began to focus on the arts, even released an album of his music titled *Your Love Keeps Me Off The Streets* (RCA, 1975), for which he used the stage name Wings Livinryte (*cough*). Bo Hopkins, who plays Sheriff Will Stewart, has also appeared in dozens of roles in his career. Horror fans should get a kick out of the actor who plays Mike in **MUTANT**, Lee Montgomery, who starred in the horror film **BEN** (1972). An interesting note about the actor that plays the school kid Billy in **MUTANT**, Cary Guffey: he previously appeared as the character Barry Guiler in the film **CLOSE ENCOUNTERS OF THE THIRD KIND** (1977). Jody Medford, who plays Holly Pierce in the film, also starred in **CHAINED HEAT** (1983). Jennifer Warren, who plays Dr. Myra Tate, is best known for her work in the films **SLAP-SHOT** (1977) and **NIGHT MOVES** (1975). The late Marc Clement (1950-1990), who played Albert Hogue the redneck slimeball in **MUTANT**, also starred in the genre flick **KING KONG LIVES** (1986).

When **MUTANT** originally ran in the movie theatres, it was titled **NIGHT SHADOWS**, but was re-titled when released onto VHS/DVD format, and that title has pretty well stuck and become official. **MUTANT**'s soundtrack was created by Richard Band, who is known for many horror film musical scores, and it was released by Perseverance Records in 2008, having been previously issued by Intrada Records in 1993.

This film may have been part of the downfall of the film company Film Ventures International; their flop of a previous film and the budget of **MUTANT** mixed with personal problems of the owner of the business Edward

A couple more gruesomely gregarious guys from the ever-growing horde of infected townsfolk in **MUTANT**

L. Montoro, who started FVI in 1968 where he produced and distributed exploitation and horror films. Some of his production work included **DAY OF THE ANIMALS** (1978), **PIECES** (1981) and **MORTUARY** (1983). By the end of his career, Montoro stole a million dollars from his own failing business FVI, and took off never to be seen again. Some believe he may have escaped to Mexico.

MUTANT was made available on a DVD released in 2005 by Miracle Pictures, and again in 2013 by Mill Creek as part of a budget-priced 3-DVD set called "12 Film Flesh Fest: Zombies Unbrained", which is the version I used for the review.

This is an underrated motion picture worthy of checking out, yet not a classic. It's a B-movie and should maybe get a bit more recognition as a zombie film than it did when it was first released in the USA back in August 1984.[6]

1984, USA. D: MARK ROSMAN, JOHN "BUD" CARDOS AVAILABLE FROM MIRACLE PICTURES AND MILL CREEK

6   Also see Eric Matthew Harvey's article "Peaches, Peanuts & Cinematic Panic: Seven of the Best Horror Films Shot in the State of Georgia", in *Weng's Chop* #5, p.115. –ed.

THE COMPANY OF WOLVES

Reviewed by Tony Strauss

"Once the bloom is gone, the beast comes out."

This odd, artful and atmospheric li'l spooker is the brainchild of English author/journalist Angela Carter and Irish filmmaker Neil Jordan, and presents us with a puzzle-box of a viewing experience, both narratively and philosophically. It is on its surface a collection of folk tales and parables filtered through a werewolf-centric perspective, offering up its own unique take on familiar tropes of the encompassing genres, but on a deeper level is a somewhat scholarly examination of sexual symbolism in fairy tales ("Little Red Riding Hood" being at the forefront, naturally), filtered through the naïve perspective of a pubescent girl's sexual awakening…all observed through the distorting mirror of a deep dream state.

Don't worry—this isn't the kind of "dream state" or "dreamlike" description sometimes given to excuse confusing or pretentious or just-plain-shitty filmmaking; the very deliberate dreamlike nature of this film is an integral part of its presentation, and one of the film's bigger successes. So calm down and keep reading.

The story, such as it is, begins with a well-to-do family living in a manor home in the modern-day (*circa* early '80s) English countryside. Mother (Tusse Silberg) and

Red-cloaked Rosaleen (Sarah Patterson) is about to learn why you should "never trust a man whose eyebrows meet" in Neil Jordan's **THE COMPANY OF WOLVES**

In this Spanish lobby card image, UK pop star Danielle Dax shows one of the sexier reasons why some folks prefer **THE COMPANY OF WOLVES** to that of people

Father (David Warner) arrive home from a trip, and the eldest of their two daughters, teenager Alice (Georgia Slow), rushes out to meet them, hoping for presents. They tell her that she must first go fetch her sister, and she indignantly obliges, angry that the little "pest" is yet again an obstacle to her plans. She knocks at her little sister's door, accusing her of stealing her lipstick again, and tells her to come downstairs. Inside the room, 12-year-old Rosaleen (Sarah Patterson) sleeps in her bed, surrounded by toys and stuffed animals, her lips shiny red with purloined lipstick and her cheeks red with rouge, dreaming deeply, undisturbed by her sister's knocking and shouting. As Alice's indignant summoning fades into the background, we enter the dream world of Rosaleen, and by extension the film proper...

We are transported to a centuries-ago, Grimm's-fairy-tale-like past, and see a terrified Alice running through a dark, surreal and foreboding forest decorated with sinister, giant-sized versions of the toys in Rosaleen's room that come alive and grab at Alice as she passes. Hot on her heels is a pack of glowing-eyed wolves, which quickly overtakes her and brings her to a toothy demise.

After her sister's funeral, old-timey dreamland version of Rosaleen goes to stay the night with her stern but kindly Granny (Angela Lansbury), who is full of country wisdom and sinister tales with important lessons. She warns explicitly of the dangers of "the beast in men", and cautions that a wolf is not always a wolf, and insists that a girl should *never* trust a man whose eyebrows meet.

As Granny knits by the fire (no prizes for guessing what iconic piece of crimson outerwear she's knitting for Rosaleen), she tells her granddaughter the tale of a young bride (Kathryn Pogson) and her new unibrowed groom (Stephen Rea), who on their wedding night are about to consummate the marriage when hubby catches sight of the moonlight is suddenly overcome with the need to answer the call of nature, so to speak. He disappears without a trace. After a time, the young woman eventually remarries and has three children. One evening while her new husband (a young, uncredited Jim Carter, lately of *Downton Abbey* and bazillions of other things) is away, Husband #1 shows up out of the blue, looking haggard and wild-eyed. And, when he sees that his wife has moved on with her life, he reacts to the betrayal by showing that he's got a real beast in him...in the most literal sense.

Granny has no shortage of home-spun warnings and tales of woe, all of which tend to lead to one unifying theme: wolves and men often tend to be one and the same—some wolves are just hairy on the inside. For instance, if a priest's bastard is born on Christmas day, feet first, with eyebrows that meet in the middle (natch), he will one day meet the Devil in the woods and be turned into a wolf. By way of illustration, we are shown such an occurrence, in which such a boy (Vincent McClaren) encounters said Devil (Terrence Stamp, in an uncredited cameo), who bestows on the boy an ointment. The boy rubs it on his chest, and immediately fur begins to grow there; the forest vines snake out and bind him in place as he howls in agony while his body transforms.

After making a memorable debut in **THE COMPANY OF WOLVES**, doe-eyed actress Sarah Patterson only ever appeared in three other films

One oft-repeated warning of Granny's is the importance of sticking to the path while traveling through the forest—which should only be done during daylight—because the moment you stray from the path, you're lost for good. On one such walk through the woods with a young village boy (Shane Johnstone) aiming for her affections, Rosaleen playfully runs away from his attempts to steal a kiss, and climbs a tree to hide. In perhaps the film's most beautifully surreal moment, she climbs high into the tree, where she encounters a crane's nest containing a hand mirror and three eggs, which all suddenly split open to reveal tiny statues of babies inside. Meanwhile, back on the ground, the amorous boy (that's actually what he's called in the script; his name is never uttered in the film) sees a freshly slaughtered cow while frantically searching for Rosaleen. Suspecting the worst, he runs back to the village to tell everyone the girl's been eaten by a wolf. While the parents of the children[7] fight, each blaming the other, Rosaleen returns. Relieved that she's safe, the men of the village decide to take no chances, and immediately form a wolf-hunting party.

While the men are away, Rosaleen relates to her mother the story of a witch woman (Dawn Archibald) who was wronged by her rich aristocrat lover (Richard Morant), when he left her with child in favor of another woman. In the most dazzlingly grotesque and memorable vignette in the film, the pregnant witch shows up unexpectedly

---

7   I find it worth noting that the boy's father is played by Brit character mainstay Brian Glover, known to most worthwhile humans as the chess-playing, joke-telling regular of The Slaughtered Lamb pub in John Landis' 1981 wolfy masterpiece **AN AMERICAN WEREWOLF IN LONDON**.

to the wedding reception, and curses everyone in attendance, watching in delight as they all begin to distend and mutate into wolves before dashing off into the forest, forever thereafter bound to sing their nightly wolf-howls to the witch and her fatherless child as a reminder of the power she holds over them. As Rosaleen finishes her story, Father returns home, white as a ghost, explaining that the wolf-hunt was successful…but when he cut off the great beast's paw to keep as a souvenir, it turned into a man's hand before his eyes!

The final dramatized cautionary tale is not a story told by Granny, but a dangerous adventure for Rosaleen herself (well, her dream incarnation, anyway…remember: the real Rosaleen is still asleep, dreaming all that we witness), in which she bundles up a basket of goodies, dons her aforementioned iconic scarlet outerwear, and sets off into the woods to visit her grandmother. On the way, she meets a handsome and sophisticated gentleman…whose eyebrows clearly and distinctly meet in the middle. He offers a challenge: if he can beat her to Granny's house, she must bestow upon him a kiss. Equally as nervous as she is enticed, she accepts the challenge. If you can't figure out where this is going, immediately contact your parents and have them re-enroll you in nursery school… but of course, even this familiar premise comes with a twist, along with one more lycanthropic tale, which you shall have to discover for yourself.

More a wound-together thematic collection of vignettes than a traditional narrative *per se*, **THE COMPANY OF WOLVES** (1984) stands alone in the werewolf subgenre, being neither fully fantasy nor horror—it's more like some form of folk-tale arthouse—while gleefully treading the grounds of both while reaching for its loftier goals as an allegorical feminist deconstruction of fairy tale symbolism. Rather ambitious for a low-budget indie flick, but it more than hits its marks on all fronts, and tackles some fairly touchy and taboo subject matter along the way. This was only Jordan's second feature, and following his debut—the gritty and realistic drama **ANGEL** (1982)—with this fantastical fare showed him to be a versatile and skilled storytelling talent rather immediately, which he has proven time and time again with such hard-and-heavy-hitters as **MONA LISA** (1986), **THE CRYING GAME** (1992), **THE BUTCHER BOY** (1997), **BYZANTIUM** (2012), among many others, from genres various and sundry.

The idea to use the fantasy/horror genres to deliver allegory for real-world sexuality is not a new one, but Jordan and Carter tread on innovative and dangerous ice by choosing to allegorize the sexual awakening of a pubescent girl in a film meant for mainstream consumption—even in the less-PC-policed era of the early 1980s. The idea could have easily blown up in their faces and alienated or offended their audience with its subtext, but they handle it with confidence and playful-yet-mature nuance, giving it just the right amount of symbolic presentation, and thankfully never falling into sexually exploitative or uncomfortable ground. In fact, they should be commended for their success on this front, as they make their messages perfectly clear without ever even coming close to sexualizing the child whose sexuality is under examination.

A child's sexual awakening is a difficult thing to deal with—I *know* I don't need to tell parents that—hell, I'm not too old to have forgotten how confusing and uncomfortable my own entry into the dreaded puberty was. Kids are curious creatures, and when their sense of sexuality begins to come to the surface, they get all kinds of weird questions and ideas into their heads, for the first time becoming aware of a world they can partially glimpse—even *feel*—but are (for good reason) effortfully shielded from for as long as possible by adults.

The film touches expertly on this sense of awakening curiosity. As Rosaleen lies in bed dreaming, her face is shown garishly made-up—a young girl's interpretation of womanhood before fully understanding the complexities and subtleties of such a state—giving her a very "tarted up" look, awkward in her effort to mature perhaps a bit too prematurely. And again, symbolically, the imagined killing of Alice can be seen as Rosaleen fantasizing her own maturation, since once there's no *big* sister, she herself can no longer be the *little* sister, and is free to move forward with the blossoming of her womanhood that she believes she wants.

In one scene, Rosaleen (dreamtime version) awakens to see her parents making love in the night. Unsure of exactly what she's witnessed, the next day she asks Mother if Father ever hurts her when they do that, because

Micha Bergese gives himself a quick bath before dinner: One of the many gruesome transformation sequences in **THE COMPANY OF WOLVES**—hooray for practical FX!

the noises Father makes sound like the noises of the beasts from Granny's tales. Forced into a conversation she's not ready to have, Mother tells her not to put all her faith in Granny's tales, for if there's a beast in men, it meets its equal in women.

Granny's constant warning to "stay on the path" couldn't be clearer in its symbolism: straying from the straight and narrow leaves a young girl vulnerable to hairy, wolf-like creatures (read: horny men) eager to lure you from the path (of righteousness/purity). Indeed, as beautiful and surreal a moment as it is, the scene in which Rosaleen finds the eggs with baby statues inside can easily be viewed as a fertility-themed

There are some things you just can't keep bottled up inside...

Totally unrelated German "Horror-Roman" utilizing images lifted from **THE VAMPIRE AND THE BALLERINA**

THE VAMPIRE AND THE BALLERINA

(*L'amante del vampiro*, a.k.a. **THE VAMPIRE'S LOVER**)

Reviewed by Steve Fenton

US ad-hooks: *"Blood-Lusting Fiend Who Preys On Girls! Vampire-Queen Who Feeds On Lifeblood Of Men! ...A company of beautiful dancers stranded in a lonely mountain village... as the horror legend two thousand years old comes alive!"*

I acquired a tantalizing preliminary glimpse into this long-elusive film via Ken Films' 200-ft. Super 8mm cut-down version (approximately 9 minutes long), which I ordered while still a teen way back in the late '70s from *Famous Monsters of Filmland*'s Captain Company merchandising dept. Having been titillated immensely by this tantalizing teaser reel, which basically functioned like an extra-long trailer and really whet my appetite for more, ever since then I had really wanted to see **THE VAMPIRE AND THE BALLERINA** (1960) in its entirety, but it was generally hard to lay eyes on for decades. Then, in 1991, care of Ted Turner's commercials-packed T.N.T. network, I belatedly realized this long-simmering minor ambition, and was happy to sit through all the commercial interruptions just to finally get to see it in something close to its entirety (yes, you better believe I fired-up the ol' VCR for the occasion!).

TVATB is yet another endearing entry in the fetishistic "jiggle 'n' jugular" vein of Italo Gothic horror melodramas, much along the lines of "Pierre King"/Piero Regnoli's **THE PLAYGIRLS AND THE VAMPIRE** (*L'ultima preda del vampiro*, 1960), Roberto Mauri's **SLAUGHTER OF THE VAMPIRES** (*La strage dei vampiri*, a.k.a. **CURSE OF THE BLOOD-GHOULS**, 1964), and the present film's director Renato Polselli's own **THE MONSTER OF THE OPERA** (*Il mostro dell'opera*, 1964). As with those other three films, our present feature **THE VAMPIRE AND THE BALLERINA** co-stars Walter Brandi in a key role. I like to think of Brandi as "The Italian Christopher Lee", albeit by way of Mexico's Germán "*El Vampiro*" Robles; even if, out of the four films mentioned here, Brandi only actually played vampires in *two* of them (i.e., **BALLERINA** and **PLAYGIRLS**), and he doesn't physically resemble either Lee or Robles—nor even a combination of the two—in the slightest.

A mysterious cloaked assailant has been committing murders throughout an unspecified countryside (presumably Transylvania by way of Italy). Considering the title, no prizes for guessing that the murders are the work of a vampire! At a nearby all-girl dance-*cum*-boarding school, most of the resident budding "ballerinas" (each and every last one of them stacked suspiciously more like moonlighting burlesque queens!) spend their time either lounging or wandering about in clingy translucent

warning against what could be the result if you stray from said path. Pretty heady stuff for a Red Riding Hood reboot!

In case you were wondering, the narrative does indeed return to Rosaleen's present-day state before the film ends, though it does so in an artfully chaotic way that offers no clean-cut closure in the way of plot, and instead merely lends weight to the idea that it's the dream that was truly important—for it's what you think and feel inside that really matter, isn't it.

If you're not on the lookout for this much heavy subtext in your werewolf movies, fear not; the film can be enjoyed entirely on a spooky fairy tale level, and there are numerous disturbing scenes of violence and horror, supported by a creative display of practical monster and transformation FX. With a solid script, a fantastic cast of faces both familiar and new, monsters and gore aplenty, and creepy fairy tale atmosphere to spare, there's really nothing to steer away from at all here (unless you're a by-the-blatant-numbers plot traditionalist, in which case, don't bother), and myriads to recommend. This one is definitely worth seeking out, especially for those who feel they've "seen it all" in the werewolf department, or those who like a little arthouse and allegory in their horror.

1984, UK. D: NEIL JORDAN
AVAILABLE FROM HENSTOOTH VIDEO
AND ITV STUDIOS

nighties. Naturally, this proliferation of giggly/jiggly, eligibly nubile "virgins" (a likely story!) attracts our hungry bloodsucker like tintacks to a magnet (I hesitate to say "like flies to horseshit"; come to think of it, perhaps "like a wasp to a honey-pot" might be a more apt analogy).

Incidentally, for alleged ballerinas-in-training, these strappingly statuesque starlets (many while dressed in impractical high heels, no less) seem to spend an inordinate amount of their class-time bumping-and-grinding along to horny stripperesque jazz/R'n'R (must be a "modern dance" course, I assume). Of course, this provides director Polselli his excuse—not that much of one was needed; this *is* Italo (s)exploitation cinema, after all!—to offer up sundry "money"-shots of wobbling post-adolescent puppy fat bulged impudently out around severely stressed leotard seams…and we can all be most thankful indeed for it! Why, in this, the "enlightened" (note quotes) era of *2 Girls, 1 Cup*, all this jolly jiggling around seen here seems positively innocuous in the extreme by comparison, which somehow makes it that much sexier…at least to me.

All the strictly two-dimensional characters mandatory to this kind of pulp-pop hokum are sketched out with the expected paucity of depth or personality: the saccharin heroine, Luisa (Hélène Rémy); the sturdy, studly hero, Luca (Isarco Ravaioli); the studious professor (Ugo Cragnani), and so on…

I won't be revealing too much if I tell you that the vampiric culprit turns out to be Herman (*Signor* Brandi), manservant to one Countess Alda (Maria Luisa Rolando), a reclusive aristocrat who dwells at the essential local "haunted castle". Herman must constantly feed on fresh human blood in order to remain handsome (by this I mean he deteriorates into a withered prosthetic boogeyman if he doesn't maintain a strict regimen of haemoglobin intake). Naturally, Luisa's desirably virginal pulchritude is soon lusted-after by the vampire, who applies the necessary neck-nibble amid a haze of volcanic erotic passion as dense as Toronto smog during a heat-wave.

The otherwise English-dubbed print aired back in the day by T.N.T. bore both the original **L'AMANTE** title, as well as the full Italian opening credits sequence, too. **L'AMANTE DEL VAMPIRO** accurately translates as "The Vampire's Lover", which accents the underlying kinky necrophilic implications far more overtly than **THE VAMPIRE AND THE BALLERINA**, its blander US release title (United Artists handled its Stateside distribution). The ultimate titillatory aspirations of the Italian title are seldom more obvious than in a discreetly implied "masturbation" scene involving the luscious Luisa's buxotic school-chum Francesca (Tina Gloriani). She "slips into something more comfortable"—namely, a filmy, bust-line accentuating nightgown (*white*, natch)— then proceeds to writhe about suggestively on her bed while anticipating the imminent advent of her nocturnal long-in-the-tooth "lover"; indeed the original uncut Italian print reportedly even goes so far as to include actual—*GASP!*—bare boobies…with *nipples*, even. It's this

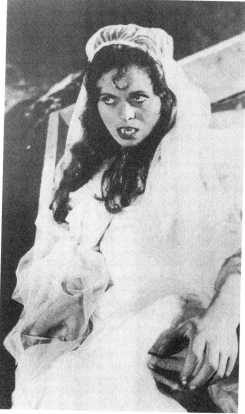

Top: Italian title card for **THE VAMPIRE AND THE BALLERINA**, which was retained even on English-dubbed US prints. **Above:** A no-longer-quite-so-sexy starlet-turned-vampiress

kind of unabashed and purely gratuitous cheezecake that oftentimes makes these movies so much more watchable, and it must have been pretty hot stuff to see 50-odd years back. Heck, it still smolders pretty nicely even in 2015!

Instilling a more subtly perverse flavor, an odd subplot depicts fanged Countess Alda feeding off the suddenly submissive Herman (once again reducing him to the

unsightly, wrinkle-faced prune he appears as throughout roughly half the running time). This unusual interdependent vampirism angle (a first for the genre?) endows an unsettlingly parasitic/sadomasochistic tone which seems apt to the fermenting sexuality of the subtext. Faint undertones of lesbianism—a vital implicit or explicit component of most post-WW2 vampire cinema—are also apparent between heroine Rémy and onscreen girlfriend Gloriani on at least one occasion. Mandatory touches of mild sexually-charged sadism help to cement all these vital sexploitative ingredients together into a satisfyingly racy whole.

The primary elements of the remaining plot involve both typical and atypical vampire film situations (e.g., Brandi drives a stake into the heart of an undead girl he has previously put the bite on; this as a means of "population control" in order to stem any unwanted multiplication of his victims). The eventual obligatory time-lapse/stop-motion "meltdown" during the climax is handled cheaply but with undoubted zeal and panache. This whole lurid passage—another given in most vampire films—best sums up the trashy appeal of these endearing '60s Italo schlockers. They are usually accused of simply being cheap monochromatic exploitations of the then-lucrative Hammer Films style, which is of course partly correct. However, to me they most bring to mind their much more analogous Mexican counterparts (e.g., Miguel Morayta's **THE BLOODY VAMPIRE** [*El vampiro sangriento*, 1962], from the same period). Like many of the Mexi-horrors, **TVATB** eschews complexities of storytelling in favor of being both picturesque and atmospheric, which is a fair trade-off as far as *I'm* concerned.

Screw nitpicking, snobbish pedants who gripe on about the superficiality or lack of redeeming qualities in such pictures. To me, naïvely naughty/sweetly saucy '50s/'60s Eurojunk like **TVATB** (similarly with Fritz Böttger's and Alex D'Arcy's vintage Teutonic T&A terror tale **BODY IN THE WEB** [*Ein Toter hing im Netz*, a.k.a. **HORRORS OF SPIDER ISLAND**, 1960]) endure as archetypical examples of a brand of dated coy cheeze-sleaze that is largely absent from screens in these jaded early years of the New Millennium. More's the pity… *[Sigh.]*

1960, ITALY. D: RENATO POLSELLI
AVAILABLE FROM NOSHAME FILMS [OOP] AND MGM [VOD]

BLOOD REINCARNATION
(陰陽界 / *Yinyang jie*)

Reviewed by Jeff Goodhartz

"Charm can do no good on ghost. You better believe it. This film is based on Cantonese legend and asks that people do good deeds."

Top: Here seen in his more presentable form, Walter Brandi prepares to put the bite on Helen Remy in **THE VAMPIRE AND THE BALLERINA**. **Center:** This is what Brandi turns into if he doesn't get his regular fix of the red stuff! **Above:** Italian poster (art by Serafini)

And with that bit of unsubtle moralizing scrolled before the title credits, we are off and running with what is widely considered the first splash of modern Hong Kong horror. Heavily influenced by 1973's **THE EXORCIST** (as were seemingly most horror movies of the period from every corner of the planet), veteran writer/director Ting Shan-Hsi crafts an amped-up experience in the manner of the trusty horror anthology. While Ting's effort may not hold up compared to the classics of this subgenre such as **DEAD OF NIGHT** (1945), **BLACK SABBATH** (*I tre volti della paura*, 1963) and **TALES FROM THE CRYPT** (1972), it's brash eclecticism makes for a worthy late-night watch.

Kicking off our trilogy (and by that I mean ripping it from its haunted hinges) is "The Treasure". On a dark and stormy night (always a good way to start these things) we witness Ah Heung (Shirley Huang) in labor and having a particularly grueling time of it. Her husband, Ah Tak (Dean Shek) seems distracted by the body of a dead old woman whose eyes won't stay shut and whose picture keeps changing. Through flashback, we see that the husband and wife helped the old woman bury a covered pot in a field. Believing it to contain treasure (when in fact, it was the bones of a loved one), they rob and kill her. As Ah Heung begins delivery, her blood drips down onto the wronged woman's corpse. This apparently allows her enraged spirit to enter the womb. Upon delivery (it's a boy!), the baby transforms into a demon that bites Ah Tak's finger off before going literally for the jugular.

Running a brief thirteen minutes, "The Treasure" goes for a max audiovisual assault and succeeds admirably. Hysterical in every sense of the word (the demon baby finale enlists gasps and unintended guffaws in equal measure), it provides a brief blast of manic energy that likely sent local audiences reeling during its initial run.

Next up is "The Wanton", another tale of haunted revenge, but presented this time with a darkly comic twist. An adulterous femme (Meng Li) enlists her lover (Yu Yang) in the murder of her husband. They do so by hitting the mild-mannered dolt over the head with a hammer before locking him in a trunk and dumping it (with him still alive and kicking) into the ocean (cute couple, these two). Upon their return home after a hard day's killing, our pair of nasties find themselves placed under a water curse; the man initially cannot stop urinating, and later both fall prey to a bottomless bathtub that appears to lead directly to the ocean (the same sea where hubby was dumped, perhaps?). Seeking spiritual assistance, our couple is advised to find the trunk and replace the metal nails with wooden ones which will help seal the angry spirit inside (never mind that the spiritual adviser looks suspiciously like the dead husband). After doing so, the couple then find themselves experiencing a shared nightmare involving their bed bleeding by the gallon. Worse still, the man gets possessed by a dog (!) and after sniffing the woman all over (which she mistakes for foreplay) he takes a nasty bite out of her.

Another short one running roughly twenty minutes, "The Wanton" continues the fast and furious pace of the pre-

Page from a Hong Kong pressbook for
BLOOD REINCARNATION

vious entry, if not quite the monstrous feel. The comedic elements are presented in a way that fits in well with the proceedings (something that many Hong Kong horrors of the following decade should have paid better attention to). It manages to walk the fine line between dark humor and horror without selling out to either. The result is a largely delicious little toxic brew. Unfortunately, the ending feels tacked on, as though everyone involved were looking to simply end the story rather than bring it to any real conclusion or proper climax. Indeed, enjoyably freaky though it was, the dog possession comes straight out of left field.

With the two manic shorts out of the way, we then settle into our main feature, the nearly hour-long "Lau Tin Sok". Here the tone shifts considerably and we're presented with a truly tragic tale, though one still linked to the same "revenge for a wronged death" theme as were the previous entries. Peter Yang Kwan (who gives a memorably subdued performance) stars as the title character, a kindly doctor who finds both his practice and personal life with his wife, child and mother interrupted by royal court messenger and executioner Chiu Hing (Chi Lien Kwei). It seems a rich madam (Wang Ting) is delusional and suffering from fainting spells. Dr. Lau's mastery of acupuncture is well-known and he is urged against his will to cancel his other patients' appointments in order to treat her. The tragedy occurs when it is discovered that the madam has been in an affair with a high-ranking official who doesn't want her to come to, for fear that she will spill the beans on their secret relationship. He sneaks into her room while the doctor is away and uses his needles to kill her, framing Lau in the process. Sentenced to death, Lau is approached by Chiu Hing, whom he has befriended (Chiu's son fell ill and Lau selflessly helped treat and ultimately cured him,

Open the door and run away!

THROUGH THE LOOKING GLASS

Reviewed by Andy Ross

even after learning of his sentence!). Unable to sway the official's decision, Chiu mentions to Lau the untested theory of the Blood Reincarnation. This process calls for Lau to face a certain direction, say his hometown aloud and having blood smeared on his chest just before the beheading. This will allow Lau to come back as a ghost for seven days which he will use to settle matters at home with his family. Problem is, he isn't really himself as he is cold to the touch, shuns the sunlight, only eats cold food and won't sleep. In the meantime, Chiu makes it his business to gather enough info to clear Lau's name and ultimately bring the guilty official (who conversely has risen in rank) to justice.

"Lau Tin Sok" seems to exist as much as anything else as a showcase for director Ting's range. Though eerie and haunting, it completely lacks the in-your-face hysteria of the preceding shorts. Instead, we have a highly emotional experience that for the most part works. The early scenes effectively portray Dr. Lau as a nearly Zen-like figure whose inner goodness is so strong that it transforms the initially gruff and careless Chiu into a remorseful ally. The post-reincarnation scenes play out with a subtle power as the once-gentle and -caring doctor now seems oddly cold and distant, causing his wife to initially feel estranged before slowly coming to the terrifying realization that her husband has returned as a ghost. Special mention should be made here of the effective makeup effects, courtesy of Lin Hung-Ying, showing Lau's slow physical disintegration as the seventh and final day of his return draws nearer. The episode does falter a bit during the climax as Ting tries too hard to tug at our emotions. The wife's weeping as she sends her husband's soul to the afterlife (they were in a hurry, as word of Lau's Blood Reincarnation spread to the villainous official who dispatched an Exorcist to take care of matters) was so prolonged and over the top that it became annoying rather than touching. Fortunately, it redeems itself in its final moments; word of the official's treachery leads to his execution. Chiu once again assists him with the reincarnation process…this time substituting pig's blood in place of the proper human variety!

Oddly unavailable on any media whatsoever (a shame considering its importance to the genre), **BLOOD RE-INCARNATION** (1974) can be seen only in a scratchy, faded fullscreen edition which is circulating through a couple of gray market stores. It deserves better.

1974, HONG KONG. D: SHAN-HIS TING

Ever since Benjamin Christensen sought to shock audiences with his rather candid depiction of the occult in **HÄXAN: WITCHCRAFT TROUGH THE AGES**, (*Häxan*, 1922), the Devil and his disciples have never been far from our collective consciousness. Whether we adhere to doctrine or not, films exploring demonology have invariably been a hit with movie-going audiences. Perhaps more prevalent in contemporary horror cinema, through **THE EXORCISM OF EMILY ROSE** (2005), **DRAG ME TO HELL** (2009) and **THE DEVIL INSIDE** (2012), the cinematic interpretation of the devil remains as popular as ever.

A throwback to the days when pornographic features were shot on film, boasted credible cast performances and possessed some semblance of a plot, **THROUGH THE LOOKING GLASS** (1976) is a curious example of how 'Seventies porn sought to merge satanic and pornographic genres. In a new age where "gonzo" porn has reduced the product to a coldly clinical experiment and where silicone enhancements, bizarre fetishes, and bodily functions have become the norm, the 'Seventies porn product is a reminder of a time when erotic cinema was considered very much to be an art form. Whilst pornography—the graphic depiction of the sexual act—has existed as long as mankind itself, the pornographic film remains a relatively recent innovation. Emerging from the "boys' club" territory of the "stag loop", the pornographic feature (as we recognize it today) first came to light via the release of Gerard Damiano's **DEEP THROAT** (1972). A rudimentary offering that (even today) remains a subject of contention, **DEEP THROAT** (besides proving implausibly lucrative) was to singularly readdress the perception of hard-core pornography.

As a decade that can lay claim to being the most innovative in film history, the 1970s were to witness the release of countless contemporary classics. Opening with the gritty drama of **THE GODFATHER** (1972) and culminating with the science-fiction horror of **ALIEN** (1979), the 'Seventies were a landmark decade for film, not least in the horror genre. As the most perfect example of a horror movie, William Friedkin's **THE EXORCIST** (1973)—a sublime study in demonic possession set against the backdrop of modern-day Washington DC—was to kick-start a trend for diabolically themed offerings. Besides the obvious—e.g., **THE OMEN** (1976), **TO THE DEVIL A DAUGHTER** (1976) and **THE SENTINEL** (1977)—the theme of demonic possession was to find an unlikely ally in the emergent realm of the "porno". Whilst sex and horror have always been (somewhat curiously) intertwined, it was only through the evolution of the porno feature that filmmakers were given an opportunity to expand on the concept.

Something of a rarity in the genre, **THROUGH THE LOOKING GLASS** was to explore the darkest aspects of sexual taboo whilst embracing the soundbites and visual traits of a mainstream horror production. Focusing on Catherine, the lady of the manor, who (some six years on) continues to mourn the loss of her domineering father, **THROUGH THE LOOKING GLASS** was to focus on past adolescent insecurities as a magnet for demonic forces. Rich and beautiful, Catherine is aloof, predisposed, and ultimately, frigid. Denying her husband his conjugal rights and emotionally distancing herself from her teenaged daughter, Catherine's inability to come to terms with her bereavement is destined to have dramatic consequences. Increasingly dependent upon medication and shutting herself off from the outside world, Catherine's reluctance to relinquish her past transports her to a realm of dark and libidinous fantasy. As the centerpiece of the film, it is an ornate mirror that provides a gateway to the hellish dimension. A family heirloom, resigned to the attic with the rest of her late father's belongings; after admiring herself in its reflective surface, Catherine unwittingly evokes a malevolent evil. A surprisingly well-made movie, **THROUGH THE LOOKING GLASS** is a study of one woman's encroaching madness, culminating with her inevitable descent into Hell. Adhering to the adage that the Devil has the power to assume a pleasing form, to Catherine that form appears as the embodiment of her deceased father. A successful man who, from what we can gather, harbored unnatural desires towards his daughter, that the evil chooses a familiar visage perfectly encapsulates the deceitful predisposition of the Devil. Promising eternal

beauty at the cost of her immortal soul, Catherine is lured away from the trappings of normality and plunged into a realm of darkness.

Whilst marketed as a porno, **THROUGH THE LOOKING GLASS** proffers a commendable balance between sex and horror and is notable for two oddly surrealist episodes. The first of these (a dream sequence) is an unabashed reference to the Mad Hatter's tea party in Lewis Carroll's *Alice in Wonderland* (1865). A portrait of bohemian excess with the cast resplendent in 19th Century costume, the scene jointly evokes the miscreant writings of the Marquis de Sade (1740-1814). Lingering in the memory long after the end-titles have rolled, when Catherine eventually succumbs to the lure of the Devil she finds herself transported to a barren other-world. A domain populated by deviant individuals, the film's depiction is very much inspired by the medieval concept of Hell. A nightmare vision of self-abuse, wanton lust and abject misery, few films have captured the depravity that **THROUGH THE LOOKING GLASS** can lay claim to. With one of its residents bemoaning Catherine's stench as she bathes in human excrement, whilst the nod to the devilish debauchery of **HÄXAN** is evident, even Christensen would have been loath to sink so low. An aspect of the film that is worth expanding upon, the production values of **THROUGH THE LOOKING GLASS** are surprisingly high. With cinematographer "Harry Flecks"/João Fernandes' stark contrasts serving to evoke the mansions permeating evil and Harry Manfredini's score deftly punctuating the visuals, it's clear that this was always going to be more than

just another "skin flick". It should go without saying, however, that not everything in **THROUGH THE LOOKING GLASS** is as professionally polished. As the leading lady, (upon whose shoulders the credibility of the story-line relies), Catharine Burgess is particularly wooden in her performance. Delivering lines in a flatly monosyllabic fashion, to assume that Burgess was cast because of her looks might not be far from the truth.

A welcome addition to any '70s porn feature, a supporting appearance from Terri Hall is yet another reminder of just how natural the actress was when facing the camera. Playing Lisa, the maid of the manor, even when resigned to folding clothes in the background, Hall illuminates every scene she appears in. Most notable for her performances in **THE TAKING OF CHRISTINA** (1976) and **THE DEVIL INSIDE HER** (1977), Hall's sultry Italian looks and balletic poise were to grace countless '70s sex productions. As the film's saving grace, however, (featuring as Catherine's father and embodiment of the demon) the scene-chomping performance of Jamie Gillis is nothing short of magnificent. An actor who happened across the porn industry after responding to an advert for male nude models, Gillis was to become one of the industry's most acclaimed performers. Whilst lacking the physical "attributes" of John "The Wadd" Holmes, Gillis was an actor first and a porn star second. A competent lead in such films as **INSIDE MISTY BEETHOOVEN** (1976)

Saucy paperback tie-in

and **WATER POWER** (1976), in **THROUGH THE LOOKING GLASS** Gillis adroitly steals the show.

Despite its pornographic label, **THROUGH THE LOOKING GLASS** remains a film of occult curiosity. By no means a film for the faint-hearted, and in a similar vein to the works of Walerian Borowcyzk, the sex in **THROUGH THE LOOKING GLASS** is darkly erotic rather than arousing. A sexually themed horror that traversed the realms of Lewis Carroll and H.P. Lovecraft, the film is a noteworthy example of pornography tailored to suit a wider audience.

1976, USA. D: JONAS MIDDLETON
AVAILABLE FROM DISTRIBPIX

DEVIL'S PASS
(a.k.a. THE DYATLOV PASS INCIDENT)

Reviewed by Tony Strauss

This movie boasts that it was "Based on a true story"—and, in a roundabout kind-of-sort-of way, a small part of it technically is—however, the proper, more accurate ballyhoo parlance would actually be "Inspired by true events", which describes the film far more accurately, as the narrative merely uses true events as its springboard for a whole new piece of fiction, rather than being an attempt to dramatize any actual occurrences *per se*. Granted, none of that really matters one squat in terms of how good or bad the film is, but it's one of those things I see often misused in films' ad- and tag-lines, and it sticks in my craw a little bit, so I tend to nitpick it. Maybe I let it affect me more than I should, but…I don't know. Leave me alone. Shut up.

At any rate, the true events that serve as the *inspiration* (ahem) for this film's plot are those surrounding the mysterious February 2, 1959 disappearance and subsequent deaths of nine experienced ski-trekkers in the northern Ural Mountains in western Russia. Commonly known as "The Dyatlov Pass Incident" (named after the group's leader, Igor Dyatlov), the circumstances surrounding the now-rather-famous incident are indeed fascinating, and offer extremely rich material for story-mining. To name but a few tantalizing tidbits:

- Originally a party of ten who set out from northernmost village Vizhai on January 27th, one member was forced to turn back on the second day due to illness. As a result, he was the only survivor.
- The group's campsite showed evidence that they had cut their way out from the inside of the tent and fled, leaving their shoes and belongings behind.
- Though most of the members were found to have died of hypothermia, three of the party died from fatal bone fractures, but had no external wounds related to these injuries.
- One member of the party was found missing her tongue, eyes and a piece of skull bone.

- Strange orange lights were reported to have been seen in the sky on February 2nd by a group of campers some distance south of the Dyatlov party.
- Unusually high levels of radiation were detected on some of the corpses, but not all of them.
- When the government's files documenting the investigation of the incident were finally declassified in 1990, several portions were missing.

This is but a sampling of the myriad baffling facts surrounding this case. Sure, there are plenty of explanations for many of them, but taken as a whole, it was and still is one helluva mystery, made ever more perplexing by the fact that no single hypothesis can seem to account for all of the evidence found at the site of the tragedy. Whatever mysterious set of circumstances brought about the team's demise we shall most likely never know, which is probably why the case has remained so popular, having inspired an endless supply of theories over the years, from those as mundane as windstorms and avalanches, to more scientific and nerdy ideas like hypothermia-induced paradoxical undressing and violent reactions to infrasonic frequencies caused by windstorm patterns, to much more "out there" explanations like UFOs and yetis…or just yer good ol' fashioned secret military cover-up.

Honestly, there's so much juicy weirdness in the incident, it's really a wonder that it took until 2013 to get a movie out of it. Sure, there've been a smattering of books (both fiction and non-), articles, and TV-investigation episodes about it here and there over the years, but no movies. That is until writer Vikram Week and director Renny Harlin came along to scoop up the idea and run with it.

DEVIL'S PASS (2013) presents itself in the form of a combination faux-doc/found-footage piece detailing the strange disappearance of a group of Oregon college students who traveled to Russia to make a documentary about the famed Dyatlov Pass Incident. We are first presented with various TV news clips reporting on the disappearance of the students and the discovery of their video camera, which the Russian government has deemed classified. We are then told that hackers obtained the footage in question and released it to the public. The remainder of the film is made up of the liberated footage which tells us the story of the students' strange fate.

Co-directors Holly (Holly Goss) and Jensen (Matt Stokoe) enlist the help of sound tech Denise (Gemma Atkinson) and expert outdoorsmen JP (Luke Albright) and Andy (Ryan Hawley) to fly to frigid northern Russia to follow the path of the ill-fated Dyatlov party in hopes of uncovering the truth of what really happened. They spend some time introducing the details of the case (a few of which the film gets wrong, but whatever) and through interview and discussion debunking many of the theories presented over the years before they gear up and set out on their trek. They have an interview arranged with the lone survivor of the party who'd turned back after the first day, who's been institutionalized after a mental breakdown, but when they arrive at the hospital the staff rudely tells them that he's passed away and orders

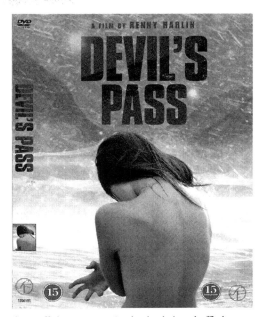

them off the property. As they're being shuffled away, they spot an old man in an upstairs hospital window holding up a sign in Russian before being pulled back by orderlies, but they have no idea what the word on the sign said. They have a sinking suspicion that the patient in the window was none other than the man they'd come to interview…but what was he trying to tell them?

That evening they have a few drinks in the same tavern in which the Dyatlov party hung out the night before they set out. After finding out about their destination and intentions, the friendly bartender serves them up a round of flaming shots, which they gratefully toss down the hatch, only to then be told that the Dyatlov party shared the same drink the night before their ill-fated journey. The group's mood suddenly takes a nose-dive, all of them having the same thoughts of bad omens. However, at the bar they also meet a nice man named Sergei (Nikolay Butenin) who offers to drive them up to Vizhai, the northernmost populated settlement from which the group set out on their skis in 1959. Sergei informs them that his aunt, who lives in Vizhai, was on the first search team to Dyatlov Pass in 1959, and she might be willing to give them an interview. Thrilled at their luck, they thankfully accept Sergei's offer. The next morning as they're piling into the back of his pickup, Holly asks Sergei to translate the word on the old man's sign…he tells her it means "stay away".

Sergei's aunt Alya (Nellie Nielsen) agrees to the interview, and informs them that when the search and rescue party arrived on the scene, they found *eleven* bodies, not nine, along with a "strange machine" lying in the snow. And, she adds, two of the bodies had "something wrong" with them.

Now more intrigued than ever, they set out on the path of the Dyatlov party, and it doesn't take but a day or so before they start to encounter strange happenings...like the bare footprints trails in the snow that seem to seem to start up and end out of nowhere...like the fact that their progress is alarmingly faster than all the maps indicate it should be...like the realization that some of the group feel a strange connection with this area...like the horrifying discovery they make inside a small weather transmitter box...

To tell you any more would be a dick move, because this is clearly a big mystery we're dealing with here, and mysteries tell their tales through the process of suspenseful revelation. What I *will* tell you is that this is a pretty damned fun mystery to pursue, filled with creepy and crazy twists and turns that run the gamut of genres. It's also a genuinely suspenseful film that uses the faux-footage medium to its advantage, rather than just trying to be gimmicky or trendy, which has been the demise of many a film of its ilk. The filmmakers applied a great attention to detail with regards to the medium serving the story and vice-versa, to the point where the presentation and the proceedings become entwined in very innovative and rewarding ways, especially with repeat viewings. Hats off to that, because that is for me something that too damned many faux-footage horror films lack: *rewatchability*. Even the more innovative and entertaining ones usually lay themselves bare with only one viewing, and avoiding that pitfall in this subgenre is a commendable achievement for this production; it's in rare company.

If I'm being completely honest, I've never been much of a Renny Harlin fan. I enjoyed **THE ADVENTURES OF FORD FAIRLANE** (1990) for what it was when it was, and I enjoyed **THE LONG KISS GOODNIGHT** (1996) mostly for Shane Black's over-the-top script, and

I...uh...thought **CUTTHROAT ISLAND** (1995) had amazing...um...poster art by Drew Struzan. But yeah, Harlin's films have never really been my thing, with all the Stallones-hanging-from-cliffs and sharky-seas-that-are-deep-and-blue and shit-awful-explody-exorcism what-have-yous; which made it all the more surprising when I got to the end of this kick-ass little flick and saw his director credit splash across the screen. Working with a much smaller budget and a smarter script seems to have brought out something special from this normally ham-fisted Finn, because the film really hit all the right notes for me, and delivered an intensely satisfying experience right up through the big whammy of an ending. Sure, it's not perfect—there's some questionable CG work involved and some of the acting gets a little stiff in one or two spots—but it never ventures anywhere remotely near deal-breaker territory.

The movie does have plenty of detractors, though, so apparently it's not for everyone's tastes. It was met with moderate interest at best upon release, drawing complaints of reimagining **THE BLAIR WITCH PROJECT** (1999) in the snow instead of the forest, disappointment for not being a dramatization of the actual tragedy, and accusations of not providing a credible solution to the Dyatlov mystery—how *dare* it! And as far as the reimagining accusation goes, I could posit that **THE BLAIR WITCH PROJECT** is a supernatural reimagining of **DELIVERANCE** (1972), which is a southern-fried reimagining of Conrad's *Heart of Darkness* (1899), which itself is a colonial jungle horror reimagining of goddamn *Alice's Adventures in Wonderland* (1865)...so there. The world is full of stories about folks who go lookin' for shit and end up findin' some other shit they wish they hadn't found...and it always will be, so relax. It's what you do

The gang poses for a group photo before their ill-fated journey to **DEVIL'S PASS**

with it that counts, right? So, bearing all that in mind and the knowledge of the large numbers of people who were butt-hurt by this film, I guess that as a responsible reviewer (*HA!*) I am obliged to pass on the "not for everybody's taste" recommendation, but I don't really see the big problem here.

In fact, you know what? Fuck it. Go out of your way to check this movie out (it's streaming on Netflix as of the time of this writing)—to hell with all the butt-hurt masses—it's a damned entertaining multi-genre flick that delivers on multiple levels and is fun to think about when it's over. In fact, I've watched it three times now and have enjoyed it a little more with each subsequent viewing. Gotta love rewatchability!

2013, USA/RUSSIA/UK. D: RENNY HARLIN
AVAILABLE FROM MPI

PADHUKAPPU

(a.k.a. **LADY KILLER** [Hindi-dubbed title])

Reviewed by Tim Paxton

As a fan of Indian cinema, I have watched over 500 of their films. That's a *lot* of mind-numbing gobbledygook, I can tell you! So there are times when I really need a film that is something which will jump out at me and get itself noticed. Last month on eBay I bought an Indian pressbook for a film called **LADY KILLER**. The front cover of this pressbook depicts a woman screaming, with the title printed large (and, yes, in English). On the back is a sexy lady in a skimpy li'l red dress, all smeared with mud. Pictured behind her is a man—covered in blood and looking pretty pissed-off—menacingly brandishing a chainsaw. These shocking images looked very different from the sorts of imagery found in most Hindi horror films from the 1990s (check out the back cover of this issue for a reproduction of the above-described). Upon seeing that image coupled with the title **LADY KILLER**, I understandably assumed I had stumbled across some Indian imitation of an Italo *giallo* or something. I thumbed through my collection of media, and sure enough, I *did* have a copy of the film on one of those insidious "3-in-1" DVD collections (meaning that the picture quality could be highly questionable: imagine shoving six hours of compressed video onto a regular 4.3GB DVD, and you'll get the picture). I had never noticed I had the film before, because all the text printed on the sleeve of the DVD is in Hindi, although the artwork with the screaming woman is the same.

Time to see what all of the fuss is about, so I popped in the DVD…

Director S.A. Chandramohan—or Chandra Mohan, as he was credited on this film—was a fairly obscure Tamil di-

Snazzy three-in-1 DVD set available at many of the Indian online store which features **LADIES HOSTEL** (a rip-off of Lucio Fulci's **DEMENTIA** of all things), **LADY KILLER**, and **PYASI APSARA**

rector from the 1990s. The fact that I have only been able to dig up information on two of his films doesn't mean that he hasn't made more. Since the 1960s, in addition to many smaller ones operating within its borders, India has boasted fully *seven* large active film industries—one for each of its states, which all have their own separate official language—and the nation as a whole produced (and still does produce) more movies per annum than any other country on Earth. While I'm not sure of the percentage, what *has* been released on video media has to be only a fraction of the total output. Much the same can be said of our own film product from the previous 100-plus years, but I would hazard a guess that we may have preserved more of our cinematic heritage than the Indians have. Apparently, preserving old films is not high on anyone's list of priorities. Yes, there is your typical mawkish sentimentality for "the classics", but when it comes to smaller films—especially those made in the despised lowbrow genres of horror, action, or thrillers—little to no notice is given to their existence. India does not have a vocal fanbase for "exploitation films" like we do in the US, UK and elsewhere. There are no openly active Kanti Shah fan clubs that I know of, although there does seem to be at least some steam building on Facebook for the recognition of the Ramsay Brothers and their horror films. But what of the thousands of shitty little movies that have been made and never properly catalogued? There is no actual Internet database for Indian films as far as I can find, and the IMDb is pretty inconsistent with whatever information they do happen to list for Indian productions (for instance, some films are listed twice in

Kollywood Klone: Pressbook art for the Tamil horror film **LADY KILLER** which is a scene-for-scene remake of American filmmaker William Freidkin's obscure 1990 druid-drama **THE GUARDIAN**. "Kollywood", like sister cinema the Bombay-based "Bollywood", is the mash-up of Kodambakkam (the cinema district of Chennai, India) and Hollywood.

the same director's filmography, alternate titles are listed as completely different films, etc). So, to find out just what films were directed by the likes of a Mr. S.A. Chandramohan, for instance, you really have to dig around online and in books (what few are available on the topic). As with Chandramohan's, there can be any number of ways that you can write out an Indian name. For instance, on the film itself and on the assorted DVDs and VCDs I have found for **LADY KILLER**, S.A. Chandramohan is listed as just Chandra Mohan. The problem is, Chandra Mohan is a combination of two very common Tamil names, and there are many Chandra Mohans to be found in the world of entertainment. They are as varied as being unit directors to best boys, and there is even the popular Tamil actor by the name of Chandra Mohan. From what I can gather, he *didn't* direct **LADY KILLER**, though!

As the film opens, we are witness to a raucous outdoor party. The partiers are boogying-down to a rockin' Bollywood beat, and there is a whole lot of flailing of arms, groping hands and shaking of the booty going on. One particular couple, Bobbi (stunning actress Abhilasha, star of P. Chandrakumar's **FRIGHT NIGHT** [1985] rip-off **BUNGALOW NO. 666** [1990]) and her boyfriend (Charan Raj), are seen making out while dancing, which shortly segues into a close-up of Bobbi's face in the throes of an orgasm. Fade out… When we fade back in again, it's the morning after the night before. The half-naked boyfriend rolls out of bed, looking around the room for his mate Bobbi, and finds her outside enjoying a sunny morning on the beach. They cuddle and coo, and she breaks the news: she's pregnant. He's all giddy, until later that night when she's like, "Nope, no sex anymore! I'm with child," whereupon he rolls over with a sour look on his mug.

He later plans their formal engagement, and asks Bobbi to meet him at special locale. My guess was that she was going to be murdered by a chainsaw. I mean, it was on the pressbook, and I assumed that her boyfriend was going to turn out to be a maniacal killer, and therefore we'd have the "lady killer" of the title. However, that's *not* how things go down… It's nighttime, and Bobbi is strolling through a roadside park full of trees and mist when a spooky voice announces that she's "the one". The wind kicks up to gale-force, and Bobbi gets caught in a weird, magical vortex of rain, dirt, and leaves. A nearby tree with motile, prehensile boughs strips her of her outer garment, and she is exposed (although not actually nekkid, natch) to the elements. A demonic entity then appears, and the young woman's head is bashed in when she is hurled against a tree trunk; she falls to the ground dead as the demon laughs. The violent storm subsides and a bolt of lightning strikes Bobbi's fallen form. She is thus resurrected—unscathed and as good as new again—from her recent traumatic "death". Instructions are given to Bobbi that she must abduct babies and bring them as offerings to the evil spirit, so off she toddles to do just that…

NOW I understood the title: Bobbi is a *lady*, and she is a *killer*; hence, **LADY KILLER**! And not only that, but this has also turned into a film with supernatural plot elements, which could well make for some interesting viewing. So far so good, and the plot progress along nicely for the next five minutes or so, whereupon things begin to become vaguely familiar. A child reads to his younger sibling out of a book. He turns the page and a pop-up graphic of a tree emerges from the pages. We then witness his parents getting ready to go out for a party. They then leave him in care of a nanny…who steals the child and disappears, only to be seen sacrificing the nipper to a huge, haunted tree. Later, the very same woman—*Hey!* That looks like Bobbi (but…)—is hired-on as nanny of their child by a young couple (Varun Raj and Sarmila).

Oh hell, it turns out that this is an unofficial remake of William Friedkin's 1990 druid-drama **THE GUARDIAN**! After that very cool beginning, I believed I was seeing something unique, but—*nope!*—it's merely another bit of Indian plagiarism. Have you even *heard* of that Friedkin film? It came and went without much of a whimper, and I found it mildly entertaining, but it doesn't even come close to the director's earlier, edgier work: the **BOYS IN THE BAND** (1970), **THE FRENCH CONNECTION** (1971), **THE EXORCIST** (1973), **SORCERER** (1977), **CRUISING** (1980), and **TO LIVE AND DIE IN L.A.** (1985). **THE GUARDIAN** certainly has some moments of unique supernatural horror, but why did Chandramohan pick *it* of all things to plagiarize?

For those of you not familiar with Indian cinema (Bollywood, Tollywood, Sandlewood, etc.), one of the main bone of contentions with Western film fans is the country's directors routinely plundering Hollywood for "their" ideas. As in the case of the present title, it's often not just some subtle nod to a favorite scene from a certain film, but rather all-out piratical plagiarism from same. As with **PADHUKAPPU** (the film's original Tamil title) with its scene-by-scene replication, theft of intellectual properties in India is seldom very subtle. Granted, I have seen most of this sort of wholesale cinematic "smash-and-grab" going on in their horror movies, as that kind of fare is what I typically watch. But after doing some further digging, it seems that this epidemic knows no bounds regarding genres, and films of any kind are "fair" game to be pillaged from.

And why is this? I had the chance to chat with one director—who shall remain anonymous—and I asked him about this type of plagiarism. His response was: "It is much easier to remake another person's film; you don't have to bother yourself to come up with anything new. It is less taxing on the brain."

That kind of lazy, apathetic attitude towards filmmaking goes far in explaining why, over the past 30 years, there have been *six* **CHILD'S PLAY** (1988) and *four* **FRIGHT NIGHT** clones, with innumerable rip-offs of **THE EXORCIST**, **THE EVIL DEAD** (1981), **THE OMEN** (1976), **A NIGHTMARE ON ELM STREET** (1984) and **PARANORMAL ACTIVITY** (2007) *et al* besides. All of those knockoffs give no credit to their source material. None whatsoever. No matter how cool I

Pilfered Pop-ups: Hey, wait a second, I've seen this somewhere before! A young Indian boy opens a pop-up book featuring a spooky tree (top), and low-and-behold something similar happened a few years prior to **LADY KILLER** in the movie **THE GUARDIAN**.

think some of those films are, it's shameful that they can get away with such artistic/aesthetic murder!

Older readers will recall the numerous Italian clones based on Hollywood blockbusters that were made back in '80s and '90s. But when the Italian film industry took a nose-dive in the '90s, so did their copies. As many as were made, quantity-wise the Italian product simply couldn't hold a candle to what is *still* being churned-out on a yearly basis in India. The main difference is that the Italians made their films not just for local consumption, but for potential export into various foreign markets too. On the other hand, the vast bulk of Indian movies made are geared strictly for domestic release, although, with the ever-growing international Hindi diaspora, these films are becoming more commonplace in Canada, the UK, and parts of Australia, France, and the USA.

Other examples of "remake madness" include the Indian version of **NAINA** (2005, D: Shripal Morakhia; a.k.a. The Pang Brothers' **THE EYE** [2002]), **THE LADIES' HOSTEL** (1993, D: Ramesh Kumar; a.k.a. Lucio Fulci's **AENIGMA** [1987]), **KUCH KUCH HOTA HAI** (1998; a.k.a. **SLEEPLESS IN SEATTLE** [1993]), **MUNNA BHAI M.B.B.S.** (2003; a.k.a **PATCH ADAMS** [1998]), **SAMAY: WHEN TIME STRIKES** (2003; a.k.a. **SE7EN** [1995]), **KNOCK OUT** (2010; a.k.a. **PHONE BOOTH** [2002]), **SADAK** (1991; a.k.a. **TAXI DRIVER** [1976])…the list is quite literally *endless.*

But back to the film at hand…

There is not much to recommend after that brief opening sequence depicting the attack on Bobbi. The remainder of **LADY KILLER** is just a carbon copy of **THE GUARDIAN**, although it is fun to compare the effects work from Friedkin's project with that of the Tamil film. In both films the killer tree is pretty ridiculous when it uses its rubbery limbs and roots to attack people. In **LADY KILLER**, as in **THE GUARDIAN**, the nanny is merely the helpless pawn of an ancient evil power, kidnapping infants to sacrifice to the monstrous tree in a nearby forest. Once the baby is killed and its blood is absorbed by the tree, images of human faces and infants appear in its bark (shades of Avery Crounse's **EYES OF FIRE** [1983], which Steve Fenton shall be discussing in the upcoming issue #24 of *Monster!* mag). This, of course, had something to do with Druids in Freidkin's film, but I'm not quite sure what the connection is in **LADY KILLER**, though animated trees inhabited by angry ghosts are very common in Indian horror films and folklore. There is a scene in **THE GUARDIAN** where the tree murders three men who have attempted to rape the nanny; which reminds me of similar animated foliage and strangling vines seen in Indian horror films.

In **THE GUARDIAN** the tree is a manifestation of evil, a supernatural entity rather than some oddball species of flesh-devouring shrub. All of the wooden monsters in Indian thrillers (at least those I have seen) are haunted trees. These are plants whose limbs or vines become by purely spiritual means—typically via possession by a ghost or demon. A classic example is the horror thriller **HATYARIN** (1991, D: Vinod Talwar)[8], wherein a beau-

tiful ghostess delivers nubile young brides to a bloodthirsty possessed tree. Less stellar (but equally fun to watch) films include loads of **EVIL DEAD** rip-offs, and even the fucked-up Indian mummy movie **KHOONI PED** (2004).[9]

These sort of monstrous trees have been attacking folks in Western cinema since the 1930s. Typically, they were mobile members of the plant kingdom that would seek out humans as food, a theme made popular by the 1962 UK sci-fi film **DAY OF THE TRIFFIDS** (D: Steve Sekely, Freddie Francis; killer plants go on the rampage after the world is bombarded by a shower of meteorites), and in **NAVY VS. THE NIGHT MONSTERS** (1966, USA, D: Michael A. Hoey; killer plants attack humans who land on an island), **BRIDES OF BLOOD** (1968, Philippines, D: Eddie Romero, Gerardo de León; living tree decapitates and kills humans who foolishly stray too close), and so forth.

In **LADY KILLER**, as in **THE GUARDIAN**, the final blood-soaked sequence comes about not because of a maniac killing young women. Both films feature a climax wherein the parents are under siege by the evil nanny, who is in desperate need of some baby blood. While Bobbi is stalking the young mother and her child in their home, our heroic dad is out in the forest, where he has taken his chainsaw and proceeds to attack the huge, haunted tree. For each limb he is able to lop from the offending plant, various bits and pieces pop off Bobbi until both evil entities are vanquished.

Of course, the only other reason to watch this film besides the silly killer tree is for Abhilasha, who does nu-

8 See *Monster!* #1, p.3

9 See *Monster!* #23, p.117

Naughty Nannies! In Freidkin's **THE GUARDIAN** the evil old-world witch Camilla is played by Jenny Seagrove (*left*) and in **LADY KILLER** it's one-time sex-pot Abhilasha (*right*) who essays the part of the Indian *daayan*, or witch.

merous semi-nude scenes. She is one lovely lady, and she apparently both "wrote" and produced **LADY KILLER**. For a brief period in the late '90s she was a hot commodity in Southern Cinema. Abhilasha was a sultry babe with big brown eyes and a lovely figure who got her start in P. Chandrakumar's Malayalam-language 1988 softcore biblical film **AADHYA PAAPOM** (*"First Sin"*). Charan Raj, who plays her jerk of a boyfriend, was comfortable playing both the lead good guy as well as the heavy. He was the evil *tantrik* in Rama Narayanan's two "Angry Goddess" films **PALAYATHU AMMAN** (2000)[10] and **RAJA KALIAMMAN** (2003)[11]. Tamil director/actor/comedian Chinni Jayanth stars as the neighbor who witness Bobbi's interaction with the tree and gets killed for it. Jayanth is still a fairly well-known comedian in cinematic circles, and, like most of the actors in this film, **PADHUKAPPU** does not appear on his official filmography (neither at Wikipedia nor IMDb).

You may ask why I even bother with something like **LADY KILLER**, if it's as bad as it sounds. But I say, "Hell, why not?!" How many of you relish watching all those horrendous SyFy flicks as guilty pleasures? Or that formulaic crap from Full Moon? I rest my case...

1995, INDIA. D: S.A. CHANDRAMOHAN
AVAILABLE FROM BOTH CAPTAIN VIDEO AND
MOSER BAER ENTERTAINMENT

HEIR

Reviewed by Tony Strauss

As nervous, middle-aged father Gordon (Robert Nolan) cryptically chats online, setting up an ominous-sounding "play date", he notices a gooey, pus-like substance secreting from his palm. Clearly this is probably something to be alarmed about, but he keeps it to himself. He takes his young teenage son, Paul (Mateo D'Ayino), on a road trip to visit Denis (Bill Oberst Jr.), who claims to be an old college mate of Gordon's, but that story doesn't come across as extremely convincing. Denis behaves friendly enough, but he's intense, intimidating and creepy as fuck; it's clear to the viewer that something shady is going on here, but Paul, being your typical smartphone-absorbed teen, doesn't really pay much mind to the boring grownups, despite the fact that Denis seems to only have eyes for him, and Gordon seems to be shitting in his pants with fear and shame. But Gordon is clearly planning on going along with whatever fucked-up plans Denis has in store for Paul. What has compelled him to willingly bring his son to this lecherous pervert's house? And what's with the weird goo leaking out of his palm?

This 14-minute short comes in creepy from the get-go and doesn't let the viewer relax for a single moment, ramping up the tension and horror steadily until the gut-puncher of an ending. Yes, *Heir* (2015) is a short film that does its job nicely.

10 See *Weng's Chop* #4, p.133
11 See *WC* #4, p.136

THE GUARDIAN

LADY KILLER

Babies In The Banyan Tree: Both films feature almost the exact demonic tree complete with human faces and bodies embedded in the bark of the haunted plant.

Skillfully written and directed by Richard Powell (*Familiar* [2012]), this is a harrowing little tale of the indoctrination of a child by predators, cleverly analogized using horror tropes in smart and effective ways that deliver the terror on multiple levels. Had this short played out its narrative in a straightforward, literal manner, the film would've likely ended up a didactic bore, regardless of how well-intentioned its message might be. But the choice to present the story in analogy, as a horror film, allows the piece to resonate the same message without feeling too obvious or preachy, in addition to offering a genuine piece of spooky entertainment. I'm trying to

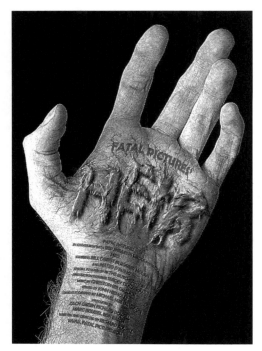

be vague here to let you discover the crazy surprises in the film for yourself…but let's just say that the horror in this film goes from Cronenbergian to full-on Yuzna before you know what hit you. And then leaves you soberly thinking about the deeper meaning well after the credits have rolled.

It's nice to finally see a growing resurgence (be it ever so slow) in the popularity—and, much more importantly, accessibility—of short films, because there are so many great ones being made every year. The short subject is an art form unto itself, quite different from feature filmmaking, and can offer a whole different set of rewards for the cinema junkie. It's films like *Heir* that help continue to breathe life into the form's popularity by demonstrating the potential of the medium. Seek this one out and watch it as soon as you get the chance. And then, once you've been thoroughly creeped out by it, watch some more shorts…I bet you'll find some goodies.

2015, CANADA. D: RICHARD POWELL
INFO AT *fatalpictures.com*

BIGFOOT CAPTURED

Reviewed by Brian Harris

As many of you have seen from some of my previous reviews on cable television programs, I am a fan of those reckless mockumentaries currently being released (i.e. **MEGALODON: THE MONSTER SHARK LIVES** [2013][12] and **MERMAIDS: THE BODY FOUND**

[2011][13]). They're irresponsible—rarely accompanied by disclaimers—and outlandish, but I find myself drawn to the P.T. Barnum of it all. Admittedly, I'm also drawn to the heated discussions surrounding these films, as well; they're hard to turn away from, like bad car wrecks featuring mutilated bodies. Dead serious here, I have seen people (online, natch!) vehemently argue the authenticity of the "facts" presented in some of these films, some even going so far as to swear they'd witnessed "monster sharks", "mermaids" and "swamp monsters" themselves. It's sad, really. I know I shouldn't derive pleasure from those that so desperately need to be seen and heard that they're willing to lie, but human frailty (including my own) fascinates me.

The History Channel—having long since given up the semblance of being interested in anything historically significant—joins Animal Planet and Discovery Channel in the deceptive freakshow with its newest mockumentary, **BIGFOOT CAPTURED** [first aired Nov. 9, 2015]. Just to establish that History Channel no longer deals in the realm of factual history, here are some of the shows currently in programming right now: *Ancient Aliens, Bible Secrets Revealed, Search for the Lost Giants* and *Pirate Treasure of the Templar Knights*. There are more; this is just a small selection of the batshit insane this channel now offers under the guise of history. It's a crying shame, but we're not here to talk about their shows, we're here to talk about…**BIGFOOT CAPTURED**. Watching this mockumentary was like walking into a bathroom just as somebody leaves, catching the full cloud of cigarette smoke and diarrhea. You knew it was going to stink; you just weren't prepared for it to be that bad.

Written by Maria and Andy Awes—the trash peddlers from Committee Films—and the debut directorial effort of Ben Krueger, **BIGFOOT CAPTURED** has a team wander into the Sierra Madre Mountains looking for Bigfoot and, big surprise here, find and capture him. No spoilers here, folks, it's in the freakin' title! I wish I could add more but there's literally nothing more to this movie than some interviews with eyewitnesses, a few sciency types talking sciency, and then the hunt itself, which consists of a few near misses and the eventual capture. There's a bit more at the finale but I'll leave that for the viewers t check out.

So, yeah…that's about it, really. Purporting to be actual footage, presented by one of the members of the group, the film is obviously a put-on, anybody that's seen even one bad movie can tell you that. Some argue that something like this shouldn't be required to feature any kind of a disclaimer because it is so obvious, but we know that people who want to believe are easily fooled. Just look how fast your family and friends share "news" proven *patently false* by websites like Snopes and PolitiFact. Consider how many of them believe memes for no other reason than they *sound* legit. All of us know somebody like that. I know I do. Thankfully, this film—unlike some of the others—offers a disclaimer…sort of.

12 See review in *Weng's Chop #4*, p.187

13 Reviewed in *WC #1*, p.8

There are scientific and eyewitness accounts that suggest a Bigfoot species could exist.

If a specimen were found it could reveal the true nature and secret history of the beast.

Portions of this program are dramatized.

Um, don't you mean all of it is dramatized? Sure they do, but this is the production company behind the not-at-all misleading productions *America Unearthed, Templars' Deadliest Secret, Holy Grail in America* and *True Monsters*. Concerned with fooling people? I'm thinking not. But you can't say there wasn't any kind of disclaimer, right?

Disclaimer or not, **BIGFOOT CAPTURED** isn't all that good. The acting was all over the place, at times ranging from quite good to "Are they serious?" Dialogue, at times, doesn't feel natural but it worked well enough to keep the production moving forward. Location, fine. The real question is, did they nail the bigfoot's visual appearance? I'd say, yes and no. He's big, hairy, intimidating and looks a bit too much like a tall dude with hair glued to his face. Is this a 2015 production or a Bigfoot film from the '70s? They should have used a bit more of the budget on special effects makeup. The one—and only—bit I found cool was a sequence featuring the captive bigfoot mournfully "singing" a haunting hominid ditty that sounds quite a bit like me after hitting the Chinese buffet.

Some mockumentaries work (**MERMAIDS: THE BODY FOUND**), while others don't (**MERMAIDS: THE NEW EVIDENCE** [2013]). **BIGFOOT CAPTURED** works as a low-budget direct-to-video B-movie, but nothing beyond that point, and even then renters may find themselves feeling a bit cheated. Honestly, I really do enjoy these films, even when they're junk—and this one was—but be forewarned, **BIGFOOT CAPTURED** offers nothing of any worth. They didn't even do a good job on the one thing that makes mockumentaries work: the documentary angle. If it

Bigfoot looks pissed! Say what you will about the production (and you'd probably be right), but **BIGFOOT CAPTURED** at the very least held its title's claim

shows up on History and you've got nothing better to do, give it a whirl. Don't go out of your way to see it though unless you're a Bigfoot film enthusiast... or a sadist, like me.

2015, USA. D: BEN KRUEGER

RATMAN

(*Quella villa in fondo al parco*, a.k.a. **RAT MAN**)

Reviewed by Michael Elvidge

French Ad-Line: "*La Cruaute' Du Rat, L'Intelligence De L'Homme...*" ("*The Cruelty of a Rat, the Intelligence of a Human...*")

I had heard of this film **RATMAN** (1988) initially back in the early '90s, in a 1990 catalogue from *Video Mania*,

Denis (Bill Oberst Jr.) entertains Gordon (Robert Nolan) and Paul (Mateo D'Avino), in *Heir*.

Mockumentary Bigfoot experts show off their track cast collection. (**BIGFOOT CAPTURED**)

a US company from Chicago, IL that sold horror VHS tapes; they carried lots of rare films you couldn't find at the local VHS rental stores. The photocopied catalogue is filled with cut-and-paste photos of films and both typed and hand-written reviews and synopsis of the movies for sale. But I couldn't afford to buy many real VHS tapes of these films at that time; I could only rent or tape films from TV.

Now, let's get to the plot of the film: it opens with scenes of rats in cages and narration from Dr. Olman (Pepito Guerra) about his creation Ratman, which is kept in a birdcage. The doctor and his assistant leave the crude laboratory…then, there is a shot of the empty birdcage—Ratman has escaped! The opening credits begin.

The film is set in the Dominican Republic, a perfect setting for a beachside photo shoot. Photographer Mark (Werner Pochath) takes photos of models Peggy (Luisa Menon) and Marilyn (Eva Grimaldi)—but someone is watching them, hidden in a nearby bush. Suddenly, Ratman springs into action, killing the peeping tom! This goes unnoticed by the trio, who continue the shoot, only to find a corpse in a rocky outcropping on the beach.

Later the models argue with Mark about reporting the corpse to the police. In the women's shared hotel room, Marilyn complains that she wants to get back to New York the following day. Meanwhile, Mark is developing the photos from that day's shoot and notices something unusual in the background of one of the photos—à la **BLOW UP** (1966)—yet this is not fully explored in the rest of the film.

At night Peggy is taking a cab to an event. The tire blows on the cab so she has to walk to her destination. She hears a noise and looks through the window of an abandoned building and sees a body being dragged away. Someone begins to pursue her and she escapes into another building. The stalker is armed with a knife and scrapes it against the walls as he approaches. Peggy hides in an abandoned wardrobe, but unfortunately her beaded necklace breaks, spilling beads and alerting the stalker to her whereabouts. But there is something in the wardrobe with her: Ratman, who squeals horribly and shreds her to ribbons! The stalker is scared off by the noise of the attack.

Fred Williams (David Warbeck) and Terry (Janet Agren) share a cab after arriving on the island by plane. Terry says she is going to a morgue, and Fred says he'll come with her. She is there to identify the body of her sister Marilyn, but it turns out be another woman, Peggy, who is carrying the ID of Terry's sister—there has been a mix up.

We learn that Fred writes mystery novels, and the police inspector tells him to mind his own business about the investigation. Fred and Terry decide to stay at the same hotel and to go to the scene of the woman's death—Fred thinks he can solve the murder with his mystery writing skills, theorizing about the possible scenarios. While at the murder scene, a cat jumps from the wardrobe and the two hide. A man enters the building, searches the wardrobe then drives off.

Next, Fred and Terry meet with the police inspector again, who has found another body, yet it isn't Marilyn either. Terry and Fred think to resolve this they should meet Mark, the photographer.

At another of Mark's photo shoots in a scenic stair-lined park, they find another woman's body. Mark, Monique

(Anna Silvia Grullon) the photographer's assistant, and model Marilyn decide to leave the scene and drive to a villa, yet it is abandoned. They decide to go back into the villa for a phone, where our little villain awaits, watching the trio, but all they find inside is devastation. Monique explores and we see Ratman pop out of a toilet and go at her. The door is locked and Mark can't help her...man, is this Ratman a ferocious little bugger!

Dr. Olman tends to Mark's wounds as he and Marilyn make their way to his house. Mark asks about the abandoned villa and what drove the people out, but the doctor seems to be deceiving Mark about what really took place. Marilyn is spied on in the shower by pervy little Ratman. Later, the two thank the doctor for helping them but as they talk they notice the little guy is there watching them in the kitchen! Olman's assistant is called into action to get his creation.

I don't want to get into any more details about the rest of **RATMAN**'s plot—you should seek it out yourself. I will say there are many scenes of action in **RATMAN**, such as eye scratching and gore! The film still emits a dark tone, as well; it isn't as humour-filled as something somewhat related film-wise, such as **LEPRECHAUN** (1993) or **GREMLINS** (1984). And there is sort of a surprise ending that you wouldn't expect. For the most part the film held my interest through it's run time. Though some might not like them I enjoy a Euro horror film every now and then.

To get back to the start of my review, here's what *Video Mania* said about **RATMAN** in their 1990 catalog…

> *"RATMAN (1989) A guaranteed stomach churner. The 'Ratman' of the title is a miniature dwarf with minimal make-up, presented as a legendary creature resulting as a cross of rat and man, who rips apart sleazy models on a Carribean island. The combination of real-life genetic mishaps, sloppy gore, cheesy nudity and exploitation of everybody involved make this one queasy experience $24.00"*

RATMAN opened to audiences on April 20th, 1988 in Italy, where it was titled **QUELLA VILLA IN FONDA AL PARCO**, and it is also known as **TERROR HOUSE** (in Germany). The film was directed by Giuliano Carnimeo, going by the name of Anthony Ascot on this film. He also directed the *giallo* film **CASE OF THE BLOODY IRIS** (*Perché quelle strane gocce di sangue sul corpo di Jennifer? / "Why are those strange drops of blood on the body of Jennifer?"*, 1972) and two spaghetti westerns **FIND A PLACE TO DIE** (*Joe... cercati un posto per morire! / "Joe... sought a place to die!"*, 1968) and **FISTFUL OF LEAD** (*C'è Sartana... vendi la pistola e comprati la bara!*, a.k.a. **I AM SARTANA, TRADE YOUR GUNS FOR A COFFIN**, 1970).

Nelson de la Rosa (1968-2006) is the actor who plays Mousey the Ratman. He was a native of the Dominican Republic and one of the shortest men on the earth at one time, measuring 2 feet 4¼ inches, he is nicknamed Mahow. Nelson did a lot of television work in foreign countries and co-starred in two other films besides **RATMAN**, **CROSS MISSION** (*Fuoco incrociato*, 1988) and the Frankenheimer-helmed **THE ISLAND OF DR. MOREAU** (1996) remake, a major studio film that bombed yet brought him lots of attention as he starred along side Marlon Brando as the character called Majai.

Actor David Warbeck is originally from New Zealand. He appeared in other genre films such as Fulci's **THE BEYOND** (*...E tu vivrai nel terrore! L'aldilà*, 1981), John Hough's **TWINS OF EVIL** (a.k.a. **THE GEMINI TWINS**, a.k.a. **TWINS OF DRACULA**, 1971), and Freddie Francis' **TROG** (1970). Janet Agren is known for horror films like Lenzi's **EATEN ALIVE!** (*Mangiati vivi!*, 1980), Fulci's **CITY OF THE LIVING DEAD** (*Paura nella città dei morti viventi*, 1980) and Richard Fleischer's **RED SONJA** (1985), where she starred as Sonja's sister Varna. Warbeck and Agren also appeared alongside each other in the film **PANIC** (*Bakterion*, a.k.a. **MONSTER OF BLOOD**, 1982).

Over this oddball film's 82-minute length, Ratman steals the show with the brief segments in which he is shown. Nelson's unique size made him perfect for the role, add some practical makeup, clawed hands and fake oversized pointed teeth, and presto: Ratman! You'll love how he scurries around, even climbing walls, hiding in small places, wardrobes, boxes, etc. Fans of actor Weng Weng will delight in seeing de la Rosa's character in action, one mean little S.O.B.

There are some good camera shots with artful appearance in **RATMAN**, and some scares, as well. Many claim this

Maybe **RATMAN** just wants a hug
...but don't bet on it!

is a horror rip-off of Sondra Locke's **RATBOY** (1986), but I can't say as I've never seen it.

RATMAN has a lot in common with other horror films with tiny villains that audiences have loved over the years, such as **CHILD'S PLAY** (1988), **GHOULIES** (1984), **CRITTERS** (1986), **LEPRECHAUN** and **GREMLINS** as I mentioned earlier, **TROLL** (1986), and a whole slew of other films. There is the B-grade factor

to this one, making sure you don't take it all to seriously, and **RATMAN** makes for some corny Euro horror entertainment that is a nice change every once in a while.[14]

1988, ITALY. D: GIULIANO CARNIMEO (A.K.A. ANTHONY ASCOT)
AVAILABLE FROM APPREHENSIVE FILMS

14 Also see Brian Harris' and George Pacheco's article "Last Gasp of a Bloodstained Industry: Italian Horror 1987-1992" in *Weng's Chop* #6, p.51 – ed.

Memoir

Written by Ben McCool / Illustrated by
Nikki Cook
Image
Cover price $3.50 (6 issues)

A Word to the Reader: You need to get the fuck on reading this! Yeah, you! Adding it to your shopping cart is a positively brilliant fucking idea! So seriously get on that! Now that we got that shit out of the way…

What if one day you woke up and had forgotten everything you knew? Your past, your family…yourself. What if your entire town woke up and had forgotten everything? Total mind fuck, right? Penetrated cerebral. Dick in the brain, if you will. They say if an event is so traumatic, so unbearable, the mind can wipe its own memory, a kind of protection from suffering so you can move on. But what kind of travesty could wipe the minds of an entire small town? That's the mystery behind Lowesville and the events that occurred there 10 years ago. No one can remember anything about themselves, or their loved ones. A whole town of strangers much worse for the unremembered wear. Quaint and friendly were lost on them a long while back. All they have had for the last decade is suspicion, surrounded by old strangers.

Like any small town in crisis, these people don't appreciate outsiders sniffing around. But Lowesville was a reporter's Twinkie cream. A town loaded with people who are all but unstitched. A gallery of Silent Hill-ish denizens. And when a reporter, name of Trent McGowan, decides to investigate the mystery behind the mass amnesia, the memories start to resurface like bloated dead bodies in the Hudson.

Trent thinks he can make it big-time with this story. He has a feeling that it will be an easy buck. A 1-2-3 job. Little does he know he's bitten off way more than he can stuff down his esophagus. Thinking this assignment will be a stroll in the park, he wanders into a sinister situation he was absolutely not fucking ready for. A mass grave, uncovered by one of the yokles. Bodies packed in the earth right on the side on the road. Every last one of them frozen in terror. Find of the century for our new reporter friend. Right as he's about to pack it in and head home he receives a mysterious email informing him that not everyone in Lowesville lost their memory. The proverbial shit slaps the spinning fan. Trent's up to his balls in one hell of a conspiracy. He can't leave Lowesville. This is too big. Little does he know that was never a fucking option.

Memoir #6 (January, 2010) by Image Comics.

Another comic rendered in my favorite color scheme: black, white, and shades of gray. Cook really captures the suspicious mood like smoke in a mirrored jar. The McCool and Cook duo is dynamic. Image is known for its heavy-hitting series, some of the best titles to ever stand shoulder to shoulder with, and outshine the titans on the comic shop shelves. And this series, like many of their myriad others, has grandiose potential of being beyond fucking amazing, landing it straight into write-mom-and-pop-back-on-the-homestead territory. This isn't your run-of-the-mill horror, either. This is more than just a few jump-and-hold-your-hearts. It has a powerful (repeat for emphasis) powerful story line. McCool's writing never skips a beat, stays in-sync, and has the tight pacing of a late-night jazz band. It drops a horizontal bar on your lap and takes you on a ride! Meeting Lowesville's strange, almost mental denizens and how they were presented worked too damn well. Paint me four shades of impressed.

Transmetropolitan #1 (July, 1997) by DC Comics/ Vertigo Comics.

I am glad I snatched this one up from issue one. The month-long wait in between issues was biblically torturous, but worth it every time one hit the shelves. The sad truth is with Image, as its titles are creator-owned, you sometimes run into a gaps in releases. In the case of *Memoir* it took *fooooooooorever* before the final issue released. Like fuckin' years if I'm remembering correctly. And to date, a trade paperback or graphic novel collecting all six issues still hasn't been released. Which is a fucking shame. Anyway, If you're still sitting here after how much time I just spent gushing about how fucking awesome this comic is…well then, what the fuck?! Go buy this! Like fucking immediately! ~ *Krys Caroleo*

Transmetropolitan

Written by Warren Ellis / Illustrated by Darick Robertson
DC/Vertigo
Cover price $14.99 - $19.99 ea. (10 volumes)

"I want to eat a swan…is that wrong of me?" – Spider Jerusalem

Cue-bald, lewd, crude, tattooed, chain-smoking, pissed off, and hot (yeah, women can objectify, too). Can you think of any other way you'd want your anti-hero? Well, you'd be wrong. I picked up the first volume, and he

wasn't staring at me, flexing his man-tits, or posing with some lame ass weapon of justice, a symbol of who gives a four-eyed, flying, shit. He was just lighting a cigarette, minding his own business. He didn't give a fuck that I was about to read his story, that I was about to discover my favorite series. That's Spider Jerusalem. He doesn't give a fuck what you think. So much so that he moved to the mountain to escape people and their cities. He thinks everyone's an asshole. And who wants to be knee-deep in asshole? Problem was…while he escaped the rat's nest of the cities, he also escaped his ability to write. A real issue for a journalist. You can't write about the trash of the world if you're not immersed in its cesspools.

When his agent (and meal-ticket) finds out he hasn't even started book one of a two-book deal after five years, Spider is called back from the mountains to the traffic-choked streets and the billboard-cluttered skylines of a city sucked up its own ass to cover the new presidential election. So it's back to the grind, back to the bowel disruptions, drug-addicted machines, dream commercials, and plastic-surgery alien junkies, all balanced with a diet of Eskimo takeout. It's cyberpunk personified. It's reality exaggerated at a thousand miles an hour. It's pissed-off on paper. It's the truth walking on water in a pair of Air Jesus shoes with a trash bag full of puppies for the children's hospital.

I love Spider. As my buddy Gord told me, "If you could 'Weird Science', one person, it would be Spider." His wit is as sharp as nails hammered into a baseball bat…one he slammed right into my heart. He sees through the users, the liars, the fakes, the swindlers, and all the scum, old and new. Spider is the foul-mouthed salty dog spitting strings of venom into a cyberpunk city gone haywire, and you love every twisted moment of him. He's torn. Complex. Conflicted. He despises people, but wants them to stand up and fight like demons for their rights even if it means taking the lesser of two assholes. Picture a tattooed, pissed off Hunter S. Thompson with a dual edge!

Darick Robertson's art perfectly captures Jerusalem's fevered, fucked-up, cluttered reality. Every character, no matter how minor, is intricately detailed. You can stare for hours, mesmerized, slack-jawed, and drooling into your lap. Not to mention this series has some of the coolest covers since the cucumber got sliced bread. We're talking "sleeve" material here. If you pick this up and don't love it right away, it's simply because you just don't get it.

A healthy, hearty, meaty mix of social political satire that keeps its action balls to the wall. In a world where even machines are drug addicts, and transplants go far past the point of being considered cosmetic, Spider is the guerilla-journalist god! This is my favorite comic series of all time. My unholy tome. The one that will stay with me forever. So if you're looking for a gonzo ride straight into the lower intestine of a futuristic metropolis, this graphic grenade will blow the lead clean out of your pencil! In the words of Biggie Smalls, "If you don't know, now you know." ~ *Krys Caroleo*

A WILDSIDE/KRONOS SNEAK PREVIEW
*film*BRAWL
by Brian Harris

As a child I was fascinated by television and films, as many people were during the 'Seventies and 'Eighties, and one of my favorite things to do was to sit down and read my mother's TV Guides. There was something about reading these little synopses that really excited me, especially when I came across a film that sounded super cool and I could remember to tune in. It wasn't until John Stanley's Creature Features Movie Guide *that I really found my passion for capsule reviews. I was hopelessly addicted to them and found myself seeking out all kinds of film books that featured them. There's just something about being able to sit down and read a few short sentences describing a film and what was good or bad about it that appealed to me. They're quick, they're easy, and they're to the point. It may sound rather lazy to some, but for people on the go in this fast-paced world, capsule reviews are actually pretty effective. They're like the fast food of the film review world. Before the Internet and film 'blogging came about, books like Stanley's and select cinema 'zines were the only way you could get your reading-lite on.*

Around the early 2000s, while working on getting my first publishing endeavor up and running, I became obsessed with the idea of crafting my own capsule review project, which I'd planned to call Joe Horror: The Guide to Blue Collar Horror. *The idea went from being a magazine to a book and back again, finally ending up as a film review website. That website eventually gave way to* WildsideCinema.com.

When I finally decided to revisit the old capsule review book idea, I settled on the name Filmbrawl *(or* filmBRAWL*). The concept was simple: throw a billion genre films into the ring and let readers fight their way through and find out for themselves which films were the winners and which were losers. As one magazine review put it, "It all smacked of an unfocused vanity project," but it was more than that to me—it was an unfocused dream project. I unceremoniously released* filmBRAWL *to Lulu around 2009/2010 and never looked back. I'd always wanted to update it and release a tighter, more focused edition, but the thought of going through the entire thing all over again to add, update and delete just felt too emotionally taxing.*

Well, it's 2015 going on 2016, and I think it's about time I took another whack at filmBRAWL *and crafted the kind of book that will be read and appreciated by film fans like me for years to come. That... and the massive amount of drugs I'm taking demand I keep moving.*

—

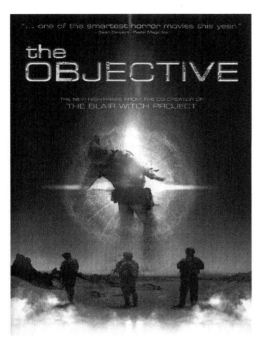

"...one of the smartest horror movies this year."

the
OBJECTIVE

THE NEW NIGHTMARE FROM THE CO-CREATOR OF
THE BLAIR WITCH PROJECT

Objective, The (2008) ★ ★ ★

A squad of soldiers is ordered to accompany a CIA operative in locating an influential Islamic cleric and securing his support for the Afghanistan war. Little does the squad know, the secretive operative is actually tracking a mysterious heat signature the government believes could be a weapon of mass destruction in the hands of the Taliban. As the group close in on the signature, strange events begin to unfold and an enemy far more powerful than the Taliban reveals itself. **The Objective** is unique and original; it's the kind of fresh, interesting and freaky sci-fi/horror I'd like to see more of. The locations were gorgeous, the production values were on-point and the antagonists, well they were flat-out terrifying. Really. If you like combat horror, with a twist of Hindu mythology, this is a must.

*Starring Jonas Ball & Matthew R. Anderson. Directed by Daniel Myrick (**Believers**).*
(DVD: 2009 / Dark Sky Films)

Onechanbara: Bikini Samurai Squad (2008) ★ ★

Zombies! Zombies! Zombies! Cowboy hat-sporting, sword-swinging, bikini-wearing Aya kicks zombie ass and takes names as she scours the countryside with her faithful and bumbling sidekick Katsuji in search of her younger sister. The fearless duo run afoul of all sorts of enemies, both zombies and human alike, and are forced to team up with a woman named Reiko, a soul just as lost seeking her own answers and revenge. The three will face many dangers and perhaps even death itself in order to reach the D3 Corporation, the insane scientist Doctor Sugita and Aya's sister. **Onechanbara: Bikini**

Samurai Squad has no socially redeeming values or artistic merit, there's barely a coherent story and the dialogue is "meh"…but folks, c'mon, there's a hot Japanese chick sword-fighting in a bikini! Really, does this have to "say" something at all? Can't it just be what it is? I say, hell yeah it can! Adapted from a Playstation 2 video game series, this is a rompin' stompin' sexy good time! It guarantees to put a smile on your face with tons of gore, nice butts galore, zombie beatdowns and some wild-ass, savage schoolgirl-on-pissed-off-bikini-samurai-girl action! The FX/CG was decent, the action was well choreographed and it's all thrown at you non-stop, kitchen sink-style. I dig it.

Starring Eri Otoguro & Taro Suwa. Directed by Yôhei Fukuda.
(DVD: 2009 / Media Blasters)

Petey Wheatstraw: The Devil's Son-In-Law (1977) ★

Do you like your blaxploitation comedies with good comedy and even better acting? Are you a stickler for dialogue? Does everything you watch have to have a plot and story? If so, don't ever, ever…*ever ever ever* watch **Petey Wheatstraw**, you filthy honky! This movie is so bad your ass will clench, toes will curl and your sides will split…from sighing to hard. Trust me, it never ends. Rudy Ray Moore plays Petey Wheatstraw, a superstar comedian with all sorts of enemies. Two in particular run a local comedy club and they're not at all amused when they learn he's slated to perform the very night they're opening their own entertainment show! They've got no other choice but to have Petey and his people executed, but they didn't count on The Devil getting involved! Old Scratch gives Petey the power to make shit happen and save his friends from death, but at a cost: Petey must marry The Devil's daughter! *OH HELL NAW!* Ugh, this is one goofy pile of kitty litter. Be forewarned, **Petey Wheatstraw: The Devil's Son-In-Law** starts out interesting, and even a little funny, but it plummets into stupidity so fast your head will spin and you'll puke pea soup. Black Judo and fine hoes can't help this garbage.

*Starring Rudy Ray Moore (**Dolemite**). Written & directed by Cliff Roquemore (**The Human Tornado**).*
(DVD: 2002 / Xenon)

Philosophy of a Knife (2008) ★ ★ ★

This four-hour graphic shockumentary details the atrocities committed by Unit 731, a research group sanctioned by the Japanese government to experiment on Chinese and Russian prisoners of war. In the same vein as **Men Behind The Sun**, **Philosophy of a Knife** drives home much of the horrendous torture and medical experimentation in all of its beautifully gory detail and never lets up for the entire run time. While ultra-violence and gore may be a fun way to blow off steam for an hour or so, **Philosophy of a Knife** slams you in the face with it over and over for four long, grueling hours. It's not entertaining, not by a long shot, but it is a unique cinematic experience which only the most devoted extreme cinema fans should attempt. If you're familiar with filmmaker Andrey Iskanov's previous films, **Nails** and **Visions of Suffering**, you know the man has an unparalleled vision rarely seen in genre cinema, and this film is quite possibly his most cohesive—and disturbing—work thus far. Those with weak stomachs, hearts and asses should avoid.

*Starring Manoush (**Barricade**), Andrey Iskanov & Irina Nikitina. Written & directed by Andrey Iskanov.*
(DVD: 2008 / Unearthed Films)

Rampage (2009) ★ ★ ★

While the world's population continues to grow and our resources dwindle, a clear choice must be made—the world needs change and we need it now. Bill Williamson, after seeing the indifference and waste, takes matters into his own hands. After stringing together an outfit of Kevlar plates and loading up several weapons, Bill sets into motion a horrifying plan to reign down chaos and mass murder on an epic scale, one that will leave dozens of bodies in its wake and the world reeling from the random insanity of it all. **Rampage** features above-average acting, interesting characters and a deeply disturbing premise that I guarantee will have people gasping. Seriously, this film might not have worked so well without the talents of such a capable cast. They all did a great job, but in the end it was Brendan Fletcher that really drove this film to its chilling conclusion; the guy can act his ass off! Uwe Boll didn't just make a "revenge film", he made a film featuring some pretty heavy ideas; issues that are currently troubling America at this very moment. It's timely as hell and very controversial. I have to say, I appreciate that. The cacophony of television and radio chatter, political and religious sound bites and divisive pundit predictions that constantly bombard us throughout the film just add an extra layer to the insanity. I found myself wondering whether we were hearing our main character's spiraling mental state or if Boll was pointing out that the whole world, not just Bill, is on a steep, rapid decline. Probably both. **Rampage** will provoke, no question. In my opinion this is a fantastic film—bravo, Dr. Boll, bravo! If you want disturbing, brutal massacre, this here is your film. If you're looking for a film that "says something", you're in luck. I highly recommend you watch it.

Starring Brendan Fletcher, Matt Frewer, Lynda Boyd, Shaun Sipos, Katharine Isabelle, Michael Paré. Directed by Uwe Boll.
(DVD: 2010 / Phase 4 Films)

Raped by an Angel (1993) ★ ★ ★

CAT III INSANITY! A sleazy, psychopathic lawyer obsessed with a young actress moves into her apartment building and rapes her roommate in order to get closer to her. Real charmer. The police are unable to do anything about him, as he's carefully covered his tracks. The target of his affection and her Triad boss boyfriend intend to see that justice is served, though! Cat III black comedy sleaze for the HK cinema fans and rape fantasy junkies. While there's a few lame laughs in this, the subject matter is deadly serious and there are a few startling sequences and a body slam finale that raises this film above the slapstick and poor English subs. Obviously this just isn't going to be for everybody, but Cat III cinema rarely is.

*Starring Simon Yam (**Election 1 & 2**). Directed by Wai-keung Lau.*
(DVD: 2001 / Tai-Seng)

Species 4: The Awakening (2007) ★ ★

Something is terribly wrong with the incredibly hot and gifted young Miranda, and whatever it is, it's causing her to kill lots of people! Her Uncle Tom flees with her to Mexico hoping to locate his long lost research partner, Forbes McGuire. Forbes may be their only hope of finding a cure for Miranda…a cure which could extend her human life and curb her homicidal alien genes! **Species: The Awakening** really isn't bad but it does suffer from a lack of backstory, spotty CG and pacing problems. One minute the film is flying at the speed of light and the next it's moving at a snail's pace. Helena Mattsson and Marlene Favela are both stunning women with beautiful racks and "hop on pop" performances. This'll probably see some cuts and end up on SyFy. Major props go to cinematographer Jaime Reynoso for his beautiful colors and imagery.

*Starring Helena Mattsson (CSI: NY), Marlene Favela (Ugly Betty) & Dominic Keating (Heroes & Enterprise). Directed by Nick Lyon (**Grendel**).*
(DVD: 2007 / 20th Century Fox)

Squeal (2007) ★ ★

A punk band on the way to a gig ends up stranded in the middle of nowhere when their van stalls on the side of the road. Instead of finding help, though, they're ac-

costed and imprisoned by a family of genetically altered mutant pig men! Wow, pig men…who woulda thunk it? Now that's a twist for ya! **Squeal** is a lowbudget amalgamation of Roth's **Hostel** and Orwell's **Animal Farm**, and just pretty fun! There are hoes with great tits, gore and…damn, people…*there are pig men!* Not only are there pig men but there is a pig midget! A pig midget that wears clownface! That's scary shit! Entertaining and original but nothing to write home about.

Starring Allison Batty, Kevin, Oestenstad, Stephen Isaac Dean & Joe Burke. Directed by Tony Swansey.
(DVD: 2008 / Simple Seed Prod.)

Tattooist, The (2007) ★ ★

Small-time ink slinger Jake, infamous for phony miracle cure tattoos, witnesses a Samoan tattoo ritual and he's immediately intrigued; unfortunately the Samoan tattooists aren't as enamored with him or his con game. Determined to incorporate their ritual into his shtick, Jake returns to the tent where the ritual took place and steals an ancient ceremonial tattoo stick. In the process, he cuts himself on it, awakening the dormant Samoan spirit that resides within it! The spirit begins killing all those Jake tattoos, leading him to believe the ghost's vendetta may lie within the Samoan tattoo community. So, Jason Behr isn't one of the greatest actors but he was able to stay awake long enough to create a not-so-perfect leading man we can relate to, which is good. The star of this flick is the Samoan spirit, though; its mannerisms and unique visuals are chill-inducing. Occasionally creepy, this J-Horror-inspired fun tastes great but is definitely less filling, it's horror-lite with bite.

*Starring Jason Behr (**Dragon Wars**), Mia Blake & Michael Hurst (Hercules: The Legendary Journeys). Directed by Peter Burger.*
(DVD: 2008 / Sony)

Tragic Ceremony (1972) ★ ★

Four hippies, given shelter during a storm, find out a little too late that their hosts are actually Satanists who plan to sacrifice one of them! Before the ritual can be completed, the three friend's bum-rush the ceremony, rescue their friend, and escape the mansion as the Satanists turn on one another in a gory frenzy! They may have escaped the clutches of the bloodthirsty devil worshipers but they haven't escaped The Devil himself! **Tragic Ceremony** starts out with potential but quickly spirals into a boring, convoluted mess of unlikable characters and unnecessary exposition. The one and only enjoyable thing about **Tragic Ceremony** is the hokey gore effects used in the "black mass massacre" sequence. Don't beat yourself up too much if you pass on this.

*Starring Camille Keaton (**I Spit On Your Grave**), Luigi Pistilli, Luciana Paluzzi & Irina Demick. Directed by Riccardo Freda (**The Iguana with the Tongue of Fire**).*
(DVD: 2008 / Dark Sky Films)

Train (2008) ★

An American college wrestling team, overseas for championship matches, is forced to ride a late train to their next destination, but this train only has one stop: death and…whatever. I'd go on but there's not much more I can offer you without giving away the entire stupid flick. Folks, I would like to officially state for the record that I am sick and tired of **Hostel** rip-offs. I love just as much gore, nudity and torture as the next horror geek, but why not try to copy a better film? This kind of crap has fizzled. American horror cinema doesn't need "**Hostel** on a train", we need filmmakers willing to take a chance on original, interesting and different cinema. Was anything in **Train** worth checking out? I could probably insist you check out some of the cool gore FX and torture sequences, a brief orgy or even Thora Birch's impression of an "Emmy-nominated corpse pretending to be an actress pretending to be a female wrestler in a shitty 'slumming it for a paycheck' horror film", but I just can't. **Train** is stupid, predictable and occasionally infuriating; there's nothing here you haven't seen before done far better. Characters are all unlikable, Birch is barely breathing and the inbred, redneck European sleazeballs are just plain silly. Pass!

*Starring Thora Birch (**Dark Corners**). Directed by Gideon Raff.*
(DVD: 2009 / Lionsgate)

ABOUT THE CONTRIBUTORS...

Stephen R. Bissette – a pioneer graduate of the Joe Kubert School, currently teaches at the Center for Cartoon Studies and is renowned for *Swamp Thing, Taboo* (launching *From Hell* and *Lost Girls*), *"1963"*, *Tyrant*, co-creating John Constantine, and creating the world's second "24-Hour Comic" (invented by Scott McCloud for Bissette). He writes, illustrates, and has co-authored many books; his latest includes *Teen Angels & New Mutants* (2011), the short story "Copper" in *The New Dead* (2010), and he illustrated *The Vermont Monster Guide* (2009). His latest ebooks are *Bryan Talbot: Dreams & Dystopias* and the *Best of Blur* duo, *Wonders! Millennial Marvel Movies* and *Horrors! Cults, Crimes, & Creepers*.

Krys Caroleo – hates umbrellas, loves poking dead things with sticks, and 34 years ago ate her twin in utero to gain its powers and become the insane yet cuddly person she is today. She is a geek, but not the kind that bites the heads off of chickens... unless they piss her off.

Michael Elvidge – hails from Durham, Ontario, Canada where he has written and illustrated several 'zines and comics since the late 1990s. He grew up loving *Famous Monsters*, horror VHS rentals, and *Deep Red* Magazine. His work has also appeared in *Monster!*, *Broken Pencil* and even art galleries. When he's not working on horror movie reviews, art and comics, he's busy hosting a weekly Internet radio show about hard rock, punk and metal music, *The Coverage Radio Show*. You can find Michael on Facebook and Tumblr.

Steve Fenton – prefers to remain as much of a mystery to others as he is to himself.

Jeff Goodhartz – is a self-righteous and self-serving man of the people who has been watching and writing about Asian Cinema for far too long. His current 'blog is *Films from the Far Reaches* (*farreachingfilms.blogspot.com* – as he's never above a shameless plug). He's quite shameless.

Brian Harris – has written for *Ultra Violent* magazine, *Exploitation Retrospect*, *Serial Killer* magazine, *Gorezone* magazine (UK) and *Hacker's Source* magazine. He's written nine books, four of which are still available, five are out-of-print. Brian has also run several websites including Joe Horror, Wildside Cinema, CineKult and Box Set Beatdown.

Christos Mouroukis – was born in Italy and has an MA in Feature Film from Goldsmiths University of London. He has directed award-winning and internationally broadcasted short films and music videos. He writes about genre movies in Greek (for *horrorant.com*) and in English (for *Weng's Chop*, *Cinema Head Cheese*, and *Monster!*). He lives in Athens with his fiancée Faye, and their cats Arte and Franco.

Louis Paul – has written for numerous fanzines and published his own, *Blood Times* (87-93). He has written several books including *Inferno Italia – Der Italienische Horrorfilm* (Bertler, Lieber, '98); *Serien Morden* (Bertler, Lieber, '00); *Film Fatales – Women in Espionage Films & Television 63-73* (McFarland, '02); *Italian Horror Film Directors* (McFarland, '05, '10); and *Tales from the Cult Film Trenches – Interviews with 36 Actors from Horror, Science Fiction and Exploitation Cinema* (McFarland, '07). Louis blames a 42nd Street double-bill of Umberto Lenzi's **ALMOST HUMAN** and the 3D porno **HARD CANDY** (with John Holmes) for disturbing his psyche for life.

Tim Paxton – lover of all things monstrous and Fortean, also has a keen interest in gardening, painting, religious iconography, and fixing old wind-up clocks. He is also keen on publishing and design, which has been keeping him busy for the past forty years.

Steven Ronquillo – is a pretentious know-it-all who looks down on his fellow film fans and refuses to reveal his faves to them unless it makes him look good.

Andy Ross – hails from Cumbria, England and recently retired from the Royal Air Force. He fell in love with film at age 9 after a trip to see Steven Spielberg's **JAWS**. In joint capacities as both an artist and a writer, Andy has worked for a number of publications, including *Little Shoppe of Horrors*, *Multitude of Movies*, *We Belong Dead*, and *Monster!* Digest magazines. While his taste in film can best be described as eclectic (everything from Borowczyck to Marvel), it is within the horror genre where his heart truly lies.

Tony Strauss – has been writing about cinema in print and online for nearly two decades. His existence as that rarest and most annoying of creatures—an artsy-fartsy movie snob who loves trash cinema (yes, it's possible)—often leaves him as the odd man out in both intellectual and low-brow film discussions. Most movies that people describe as "boring" or "confusing" enthrall him, while the kinds of movies that are described as "non-stop action" usually cure his insomnia. He has a BFA in Film, but don't hold that against him.

L. Thomas Tripp – is a longtime film fanatic and native of Las Vegas. He is currently pursuing a BA in creative writing at UNLV, and his love for film goes way back to 1985 when he first snuck in to the living room of his childhood home to watch the cable premier of the original **A NIGHTMARE ON ELM STREET**, something his mother did not want her eight-year-old son viewing. These days, not much surpasses his interest in literature, film, and writing.

Bennie Woodell – is an independent filmmaker who lives in LA and has directed seven feature films. Ever since being a kid, he's enjoyed nothing more than action, horror, and exploitation films. He loves Hong Kong Cinema and wants to one day make a film there. Until then, you can find him on-set somewhere making beautiful violence, or at the movies being inspired... mainly the New Beverly, Egyptian, or Aero Theatre in Los Angeles.

Jolyon Yates – has recently completed an 81-page WWE comic book and now considers himself an expert on drawing male nipples. He also participates in the horror movie podcast *Chewing the Scenery* (*soundcloud.com/chewing-the-scenery*).

Made in the USA
Middletown, DE
05 April 2018